NKHANZA

LISTENING TO PEOPLE'S VOICES

Copyright © 2005 GTZ

Published by
Kachere Series
P.O. Box 1037, Zomba, Malawi

ISBN 99908-76-42-8
Kachere Text no. 21

The Kachere Series is distributed outside Africa by:
African Books Collective, Oxford (orders@africanbookscollective.com)
Michigan State University Press, East Lansing (msupress@msu.edu)

Layout: Caroline Mkundi
Cover Design: Caroline Mkundi
Cover Picture: Marion Baumgart dos Santos

Printed by Lightning Source

Nkhanza

Listening to People's Voices

**A Study of Gender-Based Violence Nkhanza
in Three Districts of Malawi**

Submitted to the GTZ/Ministry of Gender and Community
Services' Project to "Combat Gender-Based Violence in Malawi

Maria Saur
Linda Semu
Stella Hauya Ndau

**Kachere Series
Zomba
2005**

Kachere Series
P.O. Box 1037, Zomba, Malawi
kachere@globemw.net
www.sdnp.org.mw/kachereseries

This book is part of the Kachere Series, a range of books on religion, culture and society from Malawi. Related Kachere titles are:

Seodi White et al., *Dispossessing the Widow. Gender Based Violence in Malawi*

Women and the Law in Southern Africa, *In Search of Justice. Women and the Administration of Justice in Malawi* (Dzuka)

Isabel Apawo Phiri, *Women, Presbyterianism and Patriarchy. Religious Experience of Chewa Women in Central Malawi*

Janet Kholowa and Klaus Fiedler, *Pa Chiyambi Anawalenga Chimodzimodzi*

Janet Kholowa and Klaus Fiedler, *In the Beginning God Created them Equal*

Andy Khumbanyiwa, *Better Days around the Corner. Restoration of Hope, Self-Confidence and the Desire to Succeed*

Andy Khumbanyiwa, *Kufa ndi Ludzu Mwendo uli M'madzi*

Harri Englund (ed.), *A Democracy of Chameleons. Politics and Culture in the New Malawi*

Bodo Immink et al., *From Freedom to Empowerment. Ten Years of Democratisation in Malawi* (gtz)

Kings M. Phiri and Kenneth Ross (eds.), *Democratisation in Malawi. A Stocktaking*

Martin Ott, Kings M. Phiri and Nandini Patel (eds.), *Malawi's Second Democratic Elections. Process, Problems, and Prospects*

The God of Love and Compassion. A Christian Meditation on AIDS

Fran Ham, *Aids in Africa: How did it ever happen?*

Chris Chisoni et al, *Dialogue between Religions. Essential Steps for Development*

Contents

List of Abbreviations

BOMA	Chichewa word for 'government and/or administration. Historically abbreviation of "British Overseas Ministry Administration"; has long been adopted into many languages for example Chichewa and Kiswahili – to mean government and or administration as it were.
GBV	Gender-Based Violence
GTZ	Gesellschaft für Technische Zusammenarbeit (German Technical Cooperation)
MHRRC	Malawi Human Rights Resource Centre
MPRSP	Malawi Poverty Reduction Strategy Paper
NPFA	National Platform for Action
NICE	National Initiative for Civic Education
UDF	United Democratic Front
TOR	Terms of Reference
MCP	Malawi Congress Party
CCAP	Church of Central African Presbyterian

Acknowledgements

First and foremost we would like to thank all our 'dialogue-partners' in the focus group discussions and in all other interviews. Wherever we went, we were most warmly received. We are most grateful and we were often moved that so much life-experience as well as most personal views and feelings about such a difficult subject were so generously shared with us! Thank you also for the feedback that all the dialogues were beneficial in a reciprocal way.

Thanks to all workshop participants they made the workshop a success.

Thanks to GTZ (Malawi) and DFID (Malawi) for funding and to MHRRC for promoting the study.

Thanks to the nuns in Dedza for taking in a stranded research team.

Thanks to Mr. Luka Mandimba our very patient driver.

Thanks to friends and families for all their support.

Last but certainly not least many thanks to our research assistants and translators: Marion Chirwa, Emmie Kumbikano and Austrida Gondwe who worked tirelessly with us under the hardest of conditions at times!

We all appreciated and enjoyed (yes, we did sing and dance a lot there) our time spent in the villages and small towns of Malawi. We were privileged to learn and understand so much about the daily life and struggle of enormously courageous and brave people, whose ability to face the hard facts of life and destiny, we can only but admire.

Our most heartfelt gratitude to all of **you**.

Yewo Chomene, Zikomo Kwambiri, Sikomo Kwejinji, Thank You Very Much

Maria Saur, Linda Semu, Stella Ndau

Preface

This booklet is based on a report which conveys the findings of a study carried out in six villages in rural Malawi, 'off the tar road' (Chambers 1996), in May/June 2003. We were to understand the social and legal status of women with the emphasis on the impact of gender-based violence. Hence group discussions and individual interviews were conducted with women, men and children from household to the Boma level.

The team applied qualitative research methods, backed up by observation through participants and statistical data collection. In order to come up with valid and reliable findings the team applied two different methods in the interviews: The so called ethno-psychoanalytical method, which was applied in the in-depth-interviews in the villages, and the 'participatory rural appraisal' approach applied in the focus group discussions.

There was striking openness in the focus group discussions and in the one to one interviews. Thus the team approach took them much beyond the realm of a base-line-study. It induced a sensitization process on a rather controversial and sensitive subject. The team was able to create fora where people could speak openly and freely about many concerns of their lives, initiating a deep process of reflection.

The research shall provide a base for a broader project to build an empowerment strategy, enabling Malawians to reflect on the subject of gender-based violence. Therefore the study was part and parcel of the implementation process for the Project to Combat Gender-Based Violence – "nkhanza kwa amayi ndi abambo".

"Nkhanza" is real in Malawi and women and men want to address this crucial issue, for change is highly desirable.

The striking difference to many other – mostly western/northern – countries is, that gender-based violence/nkhanza is openly admitted and considered by many as a 'normal' behaviour in a conflict situation between two people of any sex.

As a generally accepted behaviour "nkhanza" shall be discussed on a broader, public level hence evoke reflection, which is the foundation for change.

Change is not only on the agenda of the 'Lekani Nkhanza'- Project but also an objective of the Government of Malawi, which has signed several treaties including one on elimination of gender-based violence.

Listening to People's Voices

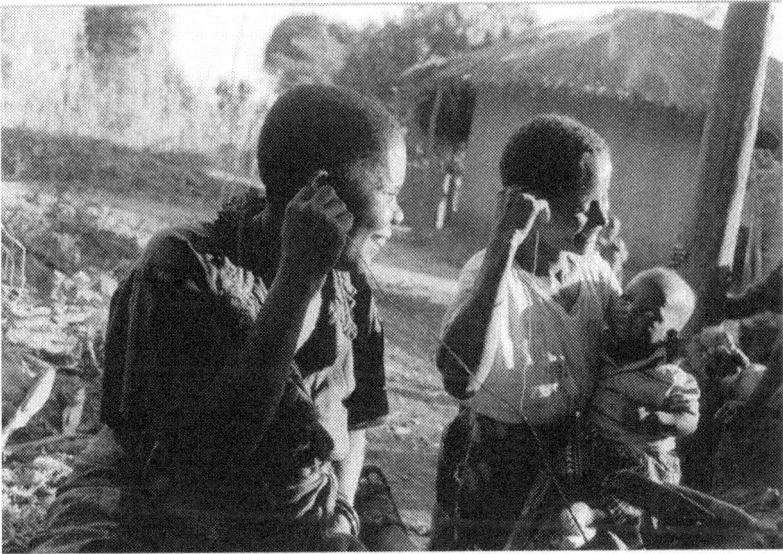

Ladies 'checking' their in-depth-interviews. Photo: Maria Saur

Focus Group Discussions: Women's' group (with Stella Ndau, Austrida Gondwe), Men's' Group (with Linda Semu, Emmie Kumbikano) in background. Photo: Marion Chirwa

Background

Background to the Study

Even though historical facts and legal rules might keep the reader from reading this book, it is at this junction necessary to give a brief background on the legal status quo of gender-based violence in Malawi: The Malawi Government is party to International and regional declarations and conventions that specify the rights of women and children. Internationally, the Malawi Government is party to: The Convention on the Elimination of All Forms of Discrimination Against Women (CEDAW, 1987) the Convention on the Rights of the Child (CRC, 1991) the Human Rights Conference in Vienna (1993); the International Conference on Population and Development in Cairo (1993); the World Summit for Social Development in Copenhagen (1994); World Food Summit in Rome (1996) and the Fourth World Conference on Women in Beijing (1995). Malawi is also a signatory to the African Charter on Human and People's Rights (ACHPR) and to the SADC Declaration on Gender and Development (1997) whose Addendum is on the "Prevention and Eradication of Violence Against Women and Children."

Furthermore Malawi was one of the 115 nations that adopted the 1995 Beijing Declaration and Platform for Action that outlines actions to be taken in twelve critical areas for human development to improve the status of women and girls. As a follow-up to the declaration, each country developed a National Platform of Action (NPFA). *The Malawi NPFA has identified the eradication of violence against women as one of four priority areas requiring an urgent response.*

A new constitution for Malawi was adopted in 1995 that includes the Bill of Rights and guarantees in Section 24 equality between women and men, women's right to property and inheritance, and invalidates any laws that discriminate against women on the basis of gender or marital status. *The provision further commits the Government to eliminate customs and practices that discriminate against women, in particular, practices such as sexual abuse, harassment and violence.*

The policy interpretation of the commitments made above has been translated into the National Gender Policy (NGP), the Malawi Poverty Reduction Strategy Paper (MPRSP), and the National Strategy to Combat Gender-Based Violence. Launched in March 2000, the National Gender Policy aims to mainstream gender in the national development process to enhance participation of men and women, boys and girls for sustainable and equitable development and poverty eradication (MOGCS, 2000). The MPRSP is the government's attempt to form a coherent framework for poverty reduction through the four strategic components of: pro-poor economic growth; human capital development; improving the quality of life for the most vulnerable; and good governance. The MPRSP further addresses gender as a cross-cutting theme through which it has incorporated as an objective the need to ensure a practical national response to gender and empowerment. It is through the latter that the Malawi Government has identified eradication of gender-based violence as one of the strategies towards attaining poverty reduction and development goals. The government also recognizes the direct negative relationship between gender-based violence and the incidence and severity of the HIV/AIDS pandemic.

Some Aspects of Malawi's Gender Profile and how they Relate to Gender-Based Violence

Gaps between women and men permeate the society at all levels. Despite forming 51% of the population, women lag behind men in all other indicators. Based on the Malawi Demographic and Health Survey, the following is a profile of the gender disparities: 72% of males are literate compared to a literacy level of 49% for women. On average, women complete three years of schooling compared to five years for men. For every population subgroup: rural - urban; northern, central and southern regions; illiterate up to secondary education, men have greater access to the mass media than women. Only 19% of women are employed all year round. The majority of women are not able to make independent decisions at the household level. Thus, for those who earn cash, only 51% are able to make independent decisions on how those earnings are to be used. A third of Malawi's households are female headed. For those women that are currently married or living with a man, the men are the major decision makers.

Household decisions	Husband only making decision
Women's health care	70.6
Large household purchases	81.3
Daily household purchases	65.7
Visits to family and relatives	36.2
What food to cook each day	42.2
Number of children to bear	42.4

Table 1: Percentage of currently married women whose husbands are the sole decision makers on major household issues. Source: Malawi Demographic and Health Survey, 2000.

Gender-based violence is widely accepted. In the Malawi Demographic and Health Survey, 35.7% of all women (22.4% for urban and 38.2% for rural) indicated that it is acceptable for a husband to beat a wife. Reasons justifying a husband beating a wife are: when she burns the food, argues with him, goes out without telling him, neglects the children, and refuses sexual relations with him. In line with cultural practices, women agree with the view that a woman has a right to refuse to have sex if she has recently given birth. However, they are less likely to agree with the view that the woman has a right to refuse sex if she is tired or not in the mood (NSO/MACRO, 2000:35). The possibility of a husband marrying a second or more wives is a lingering threat for married women. Thus, 17% of all women (19% rural and 9% urban) in Malawi are in polygamous marriages. Polygamy is more prevalent in the North, followed by the Central and Southern regions (at 26%, 18% and 14% respectively). Men prefer to have loose relationships multiple partners, thereby avoiding the formal duties that are incidental to marriage. Thus, married men are just as likely as unmarried men (20% and 21% respectively) to pay for sex.

These statistics illustrate the extent to which inequality between women and men is deeply entrenched in Malawian society. It also highlights the special challenge that a program to eradicate gender-based violence has to deal with. Gender-based violence is not only manifested as physical and/or domestic violence, but is also *structural violence that excludes women from acquisition and control over resources such as land, jobs, education, credit and other goods and services on the basis of their sex.* It is a cultural phenomenon that exists throughout the world. However, since gender roles are culturally defined, it manifests itself differently in the various cultures of the world. In and of itself, the existence of gender-based violence is an indication of the need to comprehend and overcome the unequal power relationships between women and men.

The Combating Gender-Based Violence Project and the Study

In 1998 the Ministry of Gender and Community Services requested support from the German Government for the implementation of the National Platform for Action.

In the following years a pilot project phase was undertaken during which several activities took place and research projects were undertaken. As a consequence of these activities, participants at a GTZ sponsored workshop fonded the Network Against Gender-Based Violence in 1999. The Network unites law enforcement agencies, the Ministry of Gender and Community Services, non governmental organizations, faith communities, District Administration, and other stakeholders. Based on the outcomes of the pilot phase a long-term advisory project "Combating Gender-Based Violence" was conceived. The implementation of this project started in February 2003. Its partners are the Ministry of Gender and Community Services at policy level and the Network to Combat Gender-Based violence, coordinated by the Malawi Human Rights Resource Centre (MHRRC).

The overall purpose of the project is to improve the social and legal situation of women so that they are able to independently exercise their rights.

In order to achieve the above, it became imperative that a project envisaging empowering women and men to access justice and assert their rights should be based on an exact knowledge of the cultural background, the manifestations of gender-based violence and its perception by the target-group at grass-root level. To obtain this knowledge, a qualitative baseline-study was conducted in three culturally distinct districts in Malawi: Rumphi, Dedza and Mulanje. *The knowledge acquired from this study shall then form the basis for further activities of the stakeholders and for monitoring the impact of the project.*

There is limited knowledge on gender-based violence due to the limited amount of research that has been carried out in this field. In addition, research design on gender-based violence has in the past tended to be influenced by the western received definition that limits gender-based violence to physical harm and rape. For example, Phiri & Semu's (1995) study at Chancellor College, measured the incidence of rape and sexual harassment without examining the socio-cultural context that defines the parameters of the interaction between female and male students. Similarly, Kakhongwe & Mkandawire's (1999) study is based on an analysis of rape and defilement cases for the year 1998 as recorded at six police stations, seven hospitals and five magistrate courts. While information is critical in pointing to the existence of rape and defilement abuses, it does not give us direction as to the depth of the problem and overlooks the fact that most rape and defilement cases go unreported due to lack of knowledge on existence of support structures for victims, social taboos and stigmatization, as well as inaccessibility of the services for most rural residents. It is also possible that there are other alternative avenues that are trusted and most utilized by people. All the same, the studies have raised awareness about the existence of the problem of gender-based violence and have helped people begin to talk openly about it. The Ministry of Gender's records indicate an increase in reported cases of sexual assault and domestic violence against women. Thus, the number of reported sexual assault cases against women increased from 2,500 in 1995 to 12,000 in 1999. During the same period, reported cases of domestic violence against women increased from 3,900 to 8,000 (United Nations System in Malawi, 2001).

However, it is not a matter of how much but rather the fact that gender-based violence exists that is a problem. It is therefore important to understand the process and acknowledge that one of the root causes of gender-based violence lies in the unequal power relationships between women and men. In addition, it is imperative that the socio-cultural context in which violence occurs should be understood if appropriate measures are to be taken to overcome the problem. One of the leading studies in this perspective is Chirwa's study of 1999 in which he examined "Violence and Social Injustice Against Women in the Workplace." The most significant finding of the study was that the terms violence- *Nkhanza;* unfairness– *kusowa chilungamo*; and being inconsiderate of others- *kusaganizirana* are applied to violence and social injustice. Thus, the study showed that the term *Nkhanza* is a wide concept that covers all forms of abuse; that corresponds with our findings concerning the definition of Nkhanza. However, the study was limited to the situation of women in the workplace. The current study therefore fills that gap by addressing the gender and space limitation. Thus, the Study on Gender-based Violence looked at how women, men and children define *Nkhanza.* The study concurs with Chirwa's finding that *Nkhanza* is a broad concept covering a whole range of abuses and that those abuses are based on inter-relationships among people. In addition, the study was conducted in rural areas thus giving voice to the people in the villages. The study is therefore groundbreaking as it provides us with new ways of understanding gender-based violence and new approaches to combating the problem.

Methodology

Tasks and Research Methods

The study was commissioned to examine the social, economic and legal status of women in Malawi. The main focus was therefore to capture women's, men's and children's perceptions and understanding of gender-based violence. The broad tasks. to be fulfilled were refined and grouped into two main themes. The first theme covered socio-economic data and the second theme covered issues on gender-based violence, the particular themes are covered in the section on data collection. In order to address the tasks, the team adopted three main methods of data collection: focus group discussions, in-depth interviews and key informant interviews. In addition, participant observation was utilized so as to gain a deeper understanding of the everyday experiences of the participants, particularly at the village level. Data was collected at the village and Boma (government-administration) levels. Focus group discussions and in depth interviews were utilized at the village level while key informant interviews as well as literature review and document analysis were used at the Boma level. About 1,220 people were consulted in the data collection process for this study.

Research Sites

The study was conducted in three districts of Malawi: Rumphi, Dedza and Mulanje, thus representing the three regions (North, Central and South respectively), including the ethnic and cultural diversity of Malawi. For each district two villages from two different ethnic groups were reflected. In addition, gender balance in respect to village leadership was taken as an important variable in choosing the villages. Thus in the two villages selected for each district, one was headed by a village headwoman and the other by a village headman. In Rumphi a predominantly Tumbuka village and another one that represented the ethnic diversity which is common along a major road to Tanzania, were selected. In Dedza, a Ngoni and a Chewa village were chosen while in Mulanje the villages studied were Yao and Lomwe.

District	Female Chief	Male Chief
Rumphi	Nyamaduna (Tumbuka, Phoka, and others)	Mung'anya (Tumbuka)
Dedza	Kapesi (Ngoni)	Kuluya (Chewa)
Mulanje	Kukada (Yao)	Sambatiyao (Lomwe)

Table 2: Research Villages by Sex of Village Head and Ethnicity

Data Collection

Village level

In the villages the data collection took a week using focus group discussions and in-depth-interviews. Focus group discussions were held with members of the community whereby women, men and children were met by the researchers in separate groups to encourage openness given the sensitivity of the topics. For focus group discussions, the tasks were refined into two major themes that formed the basis of discussions. The first theme was on socio-economic data through which information on activity profile of women, men and children; access to resources; control over family finances and access to social service amenities/infrastructure was gathered. The process of gathering this information also acted as a means of building rapport with the participants. This creation of trust between researchers and participants was critical for the subsequent discussions of the more sensitive themes. The second theme dealt with issues related to gender-based violence/Nkhanza in which information was solicited on: participants' perceptions of a real man and woman; discussion on the discrepancy between the ideal and reality; a discussion on what causes conflicts in families and how they are resolved; their definition of nkhanza and perceptions of the difference between criminality and nkhanza; and an evaluation of existing and possible support structures. The discussion of the second theme was often intense, and spread over two to three meetings each approximately three hours long. However, due to the rapport created earlier on, participants were able to openly discuss the sensitive issues of sexuality and nkhanza. In all villages, people expressed their gratitude for being given an opportunity to discuss such important issues as a group. They also saw the meetings as affording them a rare opportunity to get together with fellow women/men. In each village, a day was set aside for the research team to meet with young people/children and listen to their views about Nkhanza and their general socio-economic situation. In total, two weeks were spent in each District.

The in-depth-interviews were direct interview sessions with individuals in which an ethno-psychoanalytical approach was applied. Participants to the in-depth interviews were drawn from focus group discussions and were informed that it was voluntary. In order to ensure representation of in depth interview participation, sex and age were taken as important variables. In addition, the respective village headwoman or headman was one of the interviewees (dialog partners) in each village.

The methodological approach concerning interview form was as follows: the interviews were conducted in English and the local language of the villagers with the help of an interpreter.

In these interviews the dialog partner *was* empowered to take control, directing the dialog in a way that suited him or her. The intention was not to interrupt the train of thought of the interviewees thus letting them speak freely in a way that they were comfortable with and hereby letting them determine the route the conversation is taking. They clearly determine themselves when, and if at all, they want to talk about sensitive issues, in particular the sensitive issues we were most interested in like Nkhanza.

The researcher's role was to give feedback and verify if she understood what was said, to show compassion and understanding thus encouraging the interviewee to continue with his or her story in an atmosphere of mutual trust where the partner is reassured that she or he is recognised and everything that is said is valued. This approach allows for unconscious feelings, sentiments, conflicts and so far unknown motivations to surface.

As one Chief Kuluya summed it up' I learned a lot by talking with you, not that you said much, but it made me reflect on the things that have happened to us – which helped me to better come to terms with them; and maybe approach some things differently in future.'

On Boma level

The stakeholders on Boma level were individually interviewed, by one or two researchers. The researchers sought to get from the key informants the scope of their work, challenges and opportunities they encounter, and in what ways they deal with nkhanza issues in their day-to-day work. The team also evaluated from the responses the kind of networking and coordination that is already in existence at the Boma. In addition, respondents' views were solicited on how they would want to see a program to combat gender-based

In depth interview: Chief Kukada and Maria Saur. Photo: Marion Chirwa

violence operate if it were to be initiated. Documents were analyzed for trends and patterns that could be used to inform the present project. In particular, data on the incidence, nature and victims and perpetrator of gender-based violence from Police and Hospital records was collected and analyzed.

Workshop

A two-day workshop was held in which the main findings of the study were presented to all stakeholders. Thus representatives from each district where data was collected (village and Boma level), Ministry of Gender and Community Services, the Police, other stakeholders countrywide including participants from Mangochi and Kanengo where activities to combat gender-based violence supported by GTZ have been initiated, participated. The discussion was focused on the findings and strategic planning for the way forward: How Nkhanza could be tackled in Malawi?

Workshop: Mrs. Isabel Matenje, Ministry of Gender and Community Services with other participants. Photo: Maria Saur

Findings

Socio-Economic Profile

This section sets out to illustrate the macro and micro context of the economy through which women, men and children interact and from which the dynamics of gender-based violence, including perceptions on the same are played out. The survey findings on economic activities, activity profile of women and men, and access to and control over resources are presented.

Economic activities

Malawi's economy is agriculturally based, with tobacco contributing to 80% of the country's export earnings. Yet tobacco is mainly cultivated in the north. 79% of the population is in subsistence farming. Specifically, 91% and 67% of economically active women and men respectively are subsistence farmers (National Statistic Office, 2002:76). The economy grew at an impressive rate, averaging 6 % yearly growth from the time of independence in 1964 to 1979. However, the benefits of this growth did not trickle down to the population due to an agricultural policy that favoured the estate sector (tobacco/tea). A series of economic shocks: oil prices, drought and high transportation costs due to the war in Mozambique undermined the country's economic performance such that from the early 1980s, Malawi has had to implement several structural adjustment programs (Malawi Government & United Nations in Malawi: 1993). These encompassed broad-sweeping reforms. In the fiscal sector, the reforms included reduction of fiscal deficits, instituting a Treasury Bill market, private sector development policies, floating the exchange rate, initiating the stock exchange and liberalizing the banking sector. Within the agricultural sector, restrictions on burley tobacco growing were lifted and smallholder farmers could grow burley tobacco. In addition, input and commodity markets were liberalized. Public sector reforms included the privatization of companies beginning in 1996, when the privatization law was passed, and a Privatization Commission was subsequently instituted to implement the process. Within the social sector, the most significant reform has been the introduction of free primary education, with its attendant increase in the share of education expenditure in the national budget. Other social sector innovations include the establishment of the Malawi Social Action Fund (MASAF) and the introduction of a poverty monitoring system (Ngwira, et. al. 2002).

Poverty is deep and severe in Malawi. The 1998 Integrated Household Survey has shown *that 65% of Malawi's population lives below the poverty line* (National Economic Council, 2000). Agriculture is the predominant economic activity in rural areas. The incidence of poverty is higher in this sector than in the non-agricultural sector. Constraints of land, labour, food insecurity, limited access to income and credit pose as major challenges to poor subsistence farmers. Per capita land holding is lower for the poor than the non-poor. In addition, poor households have consistently lower yields than the non-poor due to their propensity to grow local rather than hybrid maize varieties. Furthermore, their incomes are irregular and tend to be 80% lower than those of the non-poor households. The poor are less likely to find employment in more secure salaried jobs. Even though almost 20% of both poor and non poor households access loans, the size of the loan differs: at MK 3,354, the mean loan size for non-poor households is nearly three times rural subsistence production, women in both joint-headed and female-headed households are likely to be poor even though the severity of poverty is more pronounced in the female-headed households.

Economic activities in the area where the survey was conducted conform to the general picture of the Malawi economy. The major economic activity for women and men in these areas is subsistence farming supplemented by agro-based trading and income generating activities. The major sources of income are presented in table 3.

Sources of Income	Mung'a nya	Nyama duna	Ka-pesi	Ku-luya	Ku-kada	Samb atiyao
Tobacco	x	x				
Basket weaving and other crafts	x	x				x
Trading in fish		x	x			
Trading in agricultural produce	x	x	x	x	x	x
Selling firewood		x	x	x	x	
Ganyu (casual labour)	x	x			x	
Employment						
Trading in wood and logs					x	
Beer brewing			x	x	x	x
Hiring out bicycle - rural transport business		F				x

Table 3: Sources of Income by Village in the Study Areas
Typical of national trends where literacy is higher in Northern Malawi, **Rumphi** has higher levels of literacy compared to the other two districts and

there is more cash income to be made due to tobacco production. Apart from tobacco, other major crops grown are: maize, sweet potatoes, bananas and cassava. Households have a wide range of livestock. Cows are usually reserved for important ceremonies and the payment of bride-wealth. Tobacco farming is a major economic activity in Rumphi and has implications on gender-based violence. Coupled with the patriarchal structure of Rumphi, gender relations at the household level operate to the advantage of men while women's labour is controlled and exploited by men. Since the men own the land, the tobacco permit is registered in their name thus all the proceeds go to them. Most men do not inform their wives of the exact amount of money realized from tobacco sales. In some cases, men take advantage of women's illiteracy and deliberately choose not to tell them the truth.

"A man can just show his wife the auction floors' print-out of tobacco sales and since the amount realized is in foreign currency, you can just tell your wife that the crop has not fetched adequate money such that you have just realized for example, MK 800.00 instead of explaining to her that it is U.S.800.00, which is much more than MK 800.00."

In addition, men squander the money by marrying new wives instead of spending it on the families with whom they produced the tobacco. Stories were narrated of men who, after getting their payment from tobacco sales, stay in rest houses at the district headquarters and do not return until all the money is used up. Some men simply marry new wives and bring them home without consulting or even informing their wives beforehand. Fair distribution of proceeds from tobacco production is clearly a point of contention and most women felt resentful about it. However, they felt that there wasn't much they could do about it since *"the land that we work on is the man's and we live in his village"*.

The propensity to abuse others through tobacco production is a major issue at the district level due to the tenancy system. Large estate owners bring in people from other districts to work as tenants on their tobacco farms. Table 4 shows the home districts of the tenants who had brought complaints to the labour office. Even though these are labour dispute issues, they can be taken as an indicator of the source of labour for the tobacco farms. Furthermore, the pattern conforms to national trends where high population growth and land shortage has resulted in the Southern region of Malawi being a source of labour for large farm owners in the Central and Northern regions. The propensity to abuse others through tobacco production is a major issue at the district level due to the tenancy system. Large estate owners bring in people from other districts to work as tenants on their tobacco farms. Table 4 shows the home districts of the tenants who had brought complaints to the labour office. Even though these are labour dispute issues, they can be taken as an indicator of the source of labour for the tobacco farms. Furthermore, the pattern conforms to national trends where high population growth and land shortage has resulted in the Southern region of Malawi being a source of labour for large farm owners in the Central and Northern regions.

In depth interview in the 'Gaffe' (tobacco drier) Chief Nyamaduna with Research Assistant/Translator Marion Chirwa. Photo: Maria Saur

Home District	Number of Complaints
Mzimba	39
Machinga	35
Zomba	30
Rumphi	29
Chitipa	25
Mulanje	24
Phalombe	23
Thyolo	15
Mangochi	14
Karonga	11
Chiradzulu	7
Blantyre	7
Ntcheu	5
Balaka	3
Dedza	2
Salima, Chikwawa, Kasungu, Mwanza, Ntchisi, Nsanje, Mchinji	1 case each

Table 4: Labour dispute issues recorded at the Ministry of Labour in Rumphi by complainant's home district, June 2001 – October 2002.
Source: Collected from Ministry of Labour Complaints Register for June 2001 to October 2002

Of the 276 recorded cases, 82% (225) had to do with wage complaints in which the majority cases were tenants facing a variety of problems from their landlords. These ranged from being chased away at or near the harvesting season, landlords inflating charges of fertilizer and other inputs, to the tenants themselves actually abandoning their families and marrying new wives during the tobacco selling season. In some cases, tenants take on new wives during the peak labour season only to chase them away at harvest time. The tenants are subject to intimidation and threats because they are not originally from the district. The Social Welfare Department in the Ministry of Gender is left with the burden of dealing with destitute tenants. The problem becomes acute during the tobacco-selling season. These problems are compounded by the fact that tenancy agreements are verbal thus it becomes difficult for the Ministry of Labour to mediate in the face of counter claims by tenants and landlords. *It is therefore important that the draft Tenancy Bill should be passed in Parliament as a matter of priority so that some of the abuses in tenancy arrangements can be overcome.*

In **Dedza** and **Mulanje**, agricultural production and a variety of income generating activities form the basis of people's income. In Dedza, irish potatoes (ordinary potatoes as opposed to sweet ones) are a critical source of income, coupled with maize and a variety of vegetables. Located close to Dedza forest, the selling of firewood is a major economic activity for women and men in the two villages. In addition, beer brewing, baking of scones, fish trading, carpentry and small-scale crafts and artisanship are sources of income. Due to poverty, some parents either abandon their children in the villages while they go to work as tenants on tobacco farms, or they send their children to work as tenants, thus creating conditions for abuse of children in both cases. Some children are also used as domestic labourers. Many urban residents come to Dedza to hire young children as domestic help without the knowledge of the labour office that would otherwise not facilitate such an arrangement since it is not legally permitted to employ anyone less than 14 years of age. Within households, children's labour is subject to exploitation by parents who expect them to carry heavy loads of wood for sale in town. Generally, the two villages in Dedza show signs of deprivation relative to the villages studied in Rumphi and Mulanje. In particular, Kuluya, situated within a 20 minute drive from Dedza town showed classic characteristics of poverty: high population as seen in too many children under-five, too many houses clustered together, poor quality clothing and signs of malnutrition. The hunger of 2001/2002 had taken a heavy toll on the village such that the level of alcohol consumption is high in both adults and children. The village is an unfortunate illustration of the failures in power relations between the government and the people, and amongst people. Men indicated that they were no longer able to provide for their families in the way they used to before *theba*, the labour migration system to the South African Mines, was abolished.

In **Mulanje**, rice production is a major source of income for some villagers in Kukada. In Sambatiyao, cassava and sweet potatoes are a viable source of livelihood. The crops were described as being their *gold*. In Sambatiyao, trading in agricultural produce involves long distance travel from the village to Mozambique where maize and other crops are bought for sale in Malawi. Being located very far from the main road and in view of limited transport facilities in rural areas, there is a thriving transport business where those individuals with bicycles hire them out. Owning a bicycle is both an indication of having accumulated wealth from the agriculture business as well as a means to acquiring income due to the demand for bicycle transportation. Farmers to some extent organize transport and sell their cassava and sweet potato produce in the markets of Limbe and Blantyre where they get better prices. However, there are no co-operatives and this is done loosely and on an individual basis in some cases. The people in this village were generally better off than those of Kukada village due to the thriving agriculture business. The velvet bean is a highly valued crop because of its drought-resistance properties. People in both Kukada and Sambatiyao described it as *mpulumutsi - saviour*, referring to the 2001/2002 famine where many had survived mainly eating this been.

The 2001/02 famine had the most severe impact in the central and southern regions compared to the northern region as presented by these narratives from Dedza and Mulanje

"In the year 2002, many people were killed due to the famine. Some farmers used to sleep in their gardens so that they could protect their crops but unfortunately not from thieves. Unfortunately, in many cases both thieves and owners of the gardens got killed in the fracas that ensued in such cases. At least things are better this year (2003)."

"Many people were dying of starvation such that at times, the gravediggers had no energy left and we usually buried all those who died on a particular day in the same grave. In some cases, people no longer had the energy to attend funerals such that in one case, a father was left to bury his child on his own."

"The government tended to provide food assistance selectively yet everybody was starving: the criteria for selecting beneficiaries on the basis of them being the elderly, orphans and the very poor did not make sense to us in the context of severe famine. In any case, the government would tell the chief to list the names of beneficiaries and yet the assistance that would eventually be brought would be cut in half."

"We used to prepare a dish of pumpkin leaves mixed with bananas. In some cases we would just make okra soup and have that as the main meal. If we were lucky, we would just buy a 'walkman'."[1]

"At the food for work program, the Clerks used to offer employment to their friends and relatives only."

"At that point, we could not even initiate sex with our wives as they would have wondered where we were getting the energy from. They would have

---

[1] Small bags of flour that are repackaged to make them affordable to the poor. They were sold in 500 gram (MK 22.00) and 1 kilogram (MK44.00) bags in the year 2002. One bag may not be adequate to prepare a full meal of *nsima* in a large family but is enough to prepare porridge. Referred to as walkman in reference to the portable radio and the fact that you can buy it as you go.

demanded an explanation from us as to whether we were having our meals somewhere else."

Access to amenities

As an additional measure of well being, the study obtained information on walking time to various social amenities (table 5). The time taken to access a particular facility depends on the location of the village: the further away from town, the longer the distance to a facility. Generally, the villages in Dedza have the least walking time to amenities, followed by the two villages in Mulanje. People of Mung'anya and Nyamaduna villages in Rumphi spend more time walking to access amenities.

Facility	Mung' anya	Nya- maduna	Kapesi	Kuluya	Kukada	Sa- mbatiao
School	1.5	2.5	0.8	0.8	0.5	0.5
Hospital	2.5	2.5	0.5	1.0	2.0	2.5
Court	2.5	3.5	0.5	2.0	2.0	4.0
Police	3.0	3.0	0.5	1.0	3.0	3.0
Market	2.5	2.0	0.8	1.0	1.0	3.0
Water Source	1.0	< .08	0.8	< 0.8	< 0.8	< 0.8
Maize mill	2.0	2.0	2.5	0.75	1.0	0.5
Grocery	2.0	2.5	< .08	< 0.8	1.0	< 0.8
Firewood	1.0	< 0.8	4.0	2.5	1.0	N/A
Garden	Nearby	Nearby	Nearby	Nearby	Nearby	Nearby

Table 5: Reported approximate average walking distance in hours to nearest facility by village

In all the three districts, people felt that the provision of loan facilities would help improve their socio-economic situation that would in turn help harmonize gender relations particularly in terms of abuse.

Things women would want to change

Reduction in fertilizer prices and provision of fertilizer loans was viewed as a priority.

"*We would like to harvest enough food crops to last from one season to the other.*"

"*We would like to be able to control our own cash because despite helping the men produce tobacco, they control the money and they use it to*

take on new wives and yet you are beaten when you ask about the money."
"For things to get better, we should be able to get cash in our own right."
"The previous government used to provide fertilizer loan facilities through farmers' clubs but now the facility is no longer there. Instead, there is the "Starter Pack" that is only provided to the elderly, orphans and core poor yet there are many people who are poor in this village."
"The price of fertilizer should be reduced and clubs for lending out fertilizer should be established."

This is also in direct reference to the government's policy changes under structural adjustment programs that had resulted in the removal of fertilizer subsidies. Farmers were in the past able to access subsidized fertilizer through farmer's clubs organized at the village level whereas now they have to access through the Malawi Rural Finance Company and other companies whose interest rates are higher.

Activity profile of women and men in households

The survey attempted to understand gender roles for women and men and how these relate to gender-based violence. The findings indicate that economic activities are linked to gender roles within households where women take up a heavy workload but have little or no control over the proceeds of their labour. There are multiple demands on women's labour, thus illustrating the critical role they play in the maintenance of household and national economies. In these villages, women and men are mostly producing their own food, goods and services and are also exchanging some of their commodities on the market for cash. While the labour demands are high for both women and men, the survey has found that women work longer hours than men (table 6). On average, men work 8-hour days, which is typical and is the accepted International Labour Organization standard. On the other hand, women have a "double shift" working on average 16 hours a day, way above the accepted international labour standard. These findings conforms to what other researchers have found. For example, Kaufulu's study (1992) found that irrespective of residence (rural vs. urban), women spend on average 16 hours working. For the low income urban woman, employment does not lead to a redistribution of household maintenance tasks. Similarly for her rural counterpart, agricultural work and household maintenance means that she has to wake up early in order to accommodate the activities of cultivating the land, food processing, childcare and housework (Kaufulu, 1992). The only exception in this study is Sambatiyao where because of the long distance trade in agricultural produce, men get up as early as two o'clock in the morning.

Table 6: Hours Spent Working by Sex and Village

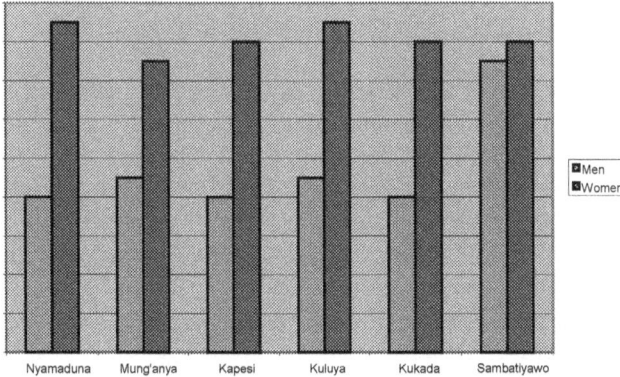

Nyamaduna   Mung'anya   Kapesi   Kuluya   Kukada   Sambatiyawo

"Timakhalira panadol"[2]: Reactions to women's working day

During focus group discussions, women and men were asked how they feel about the discrepancy in the workday. Generally both women and men feel that the labour demands on women are too much but there is a tendency to accept that as a given fact. When asked to compare with their mothers, most women felt that their mothers were better off:

> "Our mothers' lives were better because men used to commit themselves to their families and used to provide for them but nowadays all they do is drink away their money. For example, when they get money from tobacco sales, the men stay at rest houses for up to a week and when they get home and you try to inquire as to where they were, they beat you up."

> "No matter how much effort we put into farming, we still get inadequate food unlike our mothers who used to harvest enough crops"

> "The men do not participate in farm work: all they do is go beer drinking so if the woman does not work hard, the family will suffer".

> "The problem with men nowadays is drunkenness and taking on wives anyhow. This is compounded by the current freedoms unlike when we were under Kamuzu's rule, men were scared thus did not behave irrespon-sibly."

> "The problem is that when a man marries several wives, he stops working,

---

[2] Meaning: "we live on panadol"- a pain killer sold in pharmacies and groceries.

he thinks he is now the boss to control the labour but not to work."

The women expressed the hope that their daughters' lives would be better off through enhanced educational opportunities. However, they were quick to point out that even though there is free primary education, there are pressing cash needs for school supplies that they cannot afford. In addition, secondary education is not free thus quashing their hopes for moving out of the poverty cycle.

Specific reactions to their working day ranged from acknowledgement of the unfairness of it all to acceptance of the status quo:

"We live on panadols (pain-killers). Our body hurts especially when we are getting up in the morning. We have to go to the hospital at times."

"It pains us, but we can only complain about it through pounding songs."

"It is only during the first week of marriage that one is treated well. After that, you become a workhorse for the family."

"The man is the head of the family so we can't do anything about it, that's what marriage is all about."

Men acknowledged that indeed women have heavy workloads even though they tried to downplay the unfairness in the division of labour and looked for excuses for not helping.

"Women have too many things to do but their jobs are not as taxing as those that men do: you might find that a man working for a few hours will be sweating from the heavy job whereas a woman will work for long hours without sweating."

"Women have a heavier workload than men: bathing children, tilling the garden and yet when we both get home it is the woman who has to warm bath water, prepare lunch, clean up the home while as a man, we just sit on the chair. Yet after all that, when we get into bed at night, we expect her to perform the marriage contract role (sex)."

"A husband could decide to help the wife but the problem is with the women. They would in turn take advantage of you and start boasting to their friends, telling them that 'it doesn't matter even if I go home late because my husband will have done the chores.' In that instance, the women will in turn tell their husbands who will put pressure on you to conform by telling you that the woman has used a love potion so that she can control you so in the end, you just leave her to do all the chores on her own."

Access to and control over resources

In order to further verify the dynamics of the interaction between women and men, participants in focus group discussions were asked to list resources available to households, how those resources are acquired and who has control over them. Responses from women and men have been collated and the data is presented in table 7. Blanks on some items indicate that the people in that particular village did not mention that item as a resource. The data obtained on access and control over resources shows that there is a relationship between the pattern of residence and kinship structure on the one hand, and access to labour and other means of subsistence on the other. In matrilineal societies, the man acquires access to land through his wife by residing in her home and tilling her land, out of which an inherent socio-economic and political relationship emerges which is characterized by exchanges of material and emotional objects. Thus, upon marriage, a woman exchanges her land and reproductive capacity with the man's labour and reproductive capacity. The maternal uncle in this context has a relationship of authority and responsibility to allocate land while he simultaneously exercises control over his nieces and their husbands (Poeschke & Chirwa, 1998). In the patrilineal system, it is the woman who resides in the man's home and the payment of *lobola* gives her husband's family control over her productive and reproductive capacity. Irrespective of marriage system, it is clear that the common denominator in terms of access to resources is the dominance of men in family matters as well as economic and welfare issues.

Resource	Mung'anya				Nyamaduna				Kapesi				Kuluya				Kukada				Sambatio			
	M	F	J	O	M	F	J	O	M	F	J	O	M	F	J	O	M	F	J	O	M	F	J	O
Land	x				x							x	x	x			x	x			x	x		
Dimba	x					x							x						x		x			
Crops	x				x																			
Tobacco	x				x	x																		
Bicycle	x				x								x				x							x
Livestock	x	x			x					x			x	x			x				x	x		
Fertilizer	x	x			x	x	x																	
Money	x							x													x	x		
Oxcart	x							x																
Children	x				x									x				x	x		x			x
Furniture	x				x																			
Kitchen Utensils		x				x								x				x				x		
Farming Utensils							x																	
House	x				x				x				x				x				x			
Radio	x				x										x		x							x

Table 7: Sex of persons reported as decision makers and controllers of resources by village J=decisions over item made jointly; O=a person other than adult male or female in the household makes decisions.

The data in table 7 clearly shows a gender-based division on control over resources. First, it is men who dominate in decision making over the various resources at the disposal of the household. Second, women over have full control only kitchen utensils, a reflection of their roles in the household. Even in matrilineal villages, men still exercise considerable control. In the patrilineal Mung'anya village, land is out of the control of women. A woman will only exercise control if she has been allocated a piece of land to work on independently. If she gets a fertilizer loan for her garden, decisions on how to use that loan have to be made jointly since the land belongs to the husband. However, the women felt that if a marriage is monogamous, the woman participates to some extent in decision making unlike in polygynous marriages where the man makes decisions single-handedly. On the other hand, the man is not obliged to tell his wife how much money he has acquired from the sale of agricultural produce and other income sources.

The same pattern was discerned in Nyamaduna village where, in addition to fertilizer issues, joint decisions are made on produce realized from cultivation in the *dimba*, especially where the couple works on it together. In addition, joint decisions are made on how much maize to store for the family's consumption. As a rule, authority children in Rumphi district rests with the man. However, there are exceptions to this especially in cases where the woman had children outside marriage or if the *lobola* payment was not done (referred to as *"walala"*). In that instance, the woman participates in decision making over the children, together with members of her extended family.

Issues of control and decision making in the matrilineal villages studied illustrate the fluidity of culture in the face of many influences and challenges. While women are an important conduit for accessing land, its shortage has led to the growth of an informal land market in rural areas where people buy, borrow or rent land for cultivation. In most instances, it is the men who have the cash to access this form of land ownership thus they get to exercise direct control over it. Even for those who acquire land through their wives, the concept of the man as being the head of the family overrides the tradition to the extent that the men make decision on the land in terms of types of crops to be planted, how much fertilizer to apply and to which crops and how should they be sold. Just like in the north, a woman has control over the maize once it gets into the granary because it is now assumed to be for the family's consumption. Overall, there is agreement that it is the man that should control resources at the household level as observed in the following quotes:

"The fact that you are living in your wife's village does not take away your authority as a man – you still have power."
"The head of the family is still the man even though one is living under chikamwini system."
"The man is like a driver, he should determine how the family's resources are to be used".
"Wealth is best preserved with rules and those rules come from a man."
"No matter how old they get, women's intelligence is not at the same level as that of men. They have low thinking capacity."
"Women do not know how to plan."
"Women are like trailers while the man is the truck driver so we have to control the resources."
"Women's farming roles are on a part-time basis whereas for us men, we farm on a full-time basis so there is no way the woman can reprimand us for not using money prudently."
"If we were to have a joint account with our wives, they could easily kill us just so they can take full control of the money."

The seriousness surrounding a woman's decision to slaughter a chicken without first consulting her husband best illustrates the degree of male control over household resources.

"A wife is considered to have broken the rules if she slaughters a chicken without first asking the husband. You can even slap her so that she should not do it again.
"A woman cannot slaughter a chicken while you are away – one can even throw away the cooked chicken in anger."
"Before we slaughter a chicken, we have to ask for permission from our husbands, even if the chicken belongs to us."

It is clear that food is a political game revolving around issues of control. The chicken has symbolic and utility functions that are highly valued by the people: Apart from being used as relish, a chicken is used for traditional medicine procedures; is used to pay fines; can be used as a medium of exchange; and as a sign of strong friendship as noted by the following:

"A chicken is useful as a test of the strength of a friendship. If I go visit my friend and I'm given beef, it is not a big deal. However, if a chicken is slaughtered for me, I will consider that as a special welcome and that helps consolidate a friendship"

Decision-making on children is an area of contention in the matrilineal areas. In Kukada and Sambatiyao, men particularly feel impotent on their inability to exercise as much control over their children as they would want to:

"Your wife's uncle makes major decisions on the children regarding marriage and death. Your role as a father is simply to bring them up properly.

"A man and his wife raise the kids and provides for their day to day needs and yet the uncle plays a major role when it comes to important issues such as death and marriage."

"When your daughter is getting married, the man does not approach you as the father to initiate marriage proceedings. Rather, he approaches the uncle who simply informs you of the decision. You have no say as a father because if you insist that your daughter should not get married, then you are accused of having an affair with her."

Woman in Kukada drying Maize. Photo: Maria Saur

Social Structure

Marriage systems/residence patterns

This section discusses the traditional family structure of the study areas. The discussion will mainly centre on marriage and residence patterns. Generally, two types of marriage are practised: The patrilineal and matrilineal one.

For Rumphi, a patrilineal marriage system is followed. In this type of custom, the man's village is the matrimonial home and the husband is the overall authority over the family. Bride wealth (*lobola*) is paid. Nowadays they often do not pay the wealth all at once. The husband's relatives wait to analyse the woman's behaviour and also to see if she is able to have children. In case of divorce, children are left in father's custody unless the man did not pay *lobola*. Upon death of the husband, the woman has two choices either to get married to a brother in-law or to go back to her village.

Polygamy is highly practised with men marrying as many as three women as long as they are able to pay *lobola* for them. If the women live in the same village, they either stay in different houses or in the same house with different bedrooms. The study also found that there are some cases where the women share a single bedroom. Since the women live together there are many sources of tension, which yield conflicts among them and the husband respectively. If a man marries more than one wife, he is supposed to help all of them in the gardens/ fields. Some of the men stop cultivating the land and rely on the women to do the job for them. It was learnt that the men love the one who works very hard in the field.

Dedza and Mulanje districts are largely matrilineal (*Chikamwini*) with some traces of *Chitengwa*. The husband lives in the wife's village and has access to farmland through the woman's family. This practice is called *chikamwini* and the man is called mkamwini (*ndi kamwini* or *n'kamwini* which means that which belongs to someone else i.e. the husband does not belong to his wife's village, he is there solely for the marriage). Women group (maternal sisters and their daughters) are called *mbumba* and they live under the control of their maternal uncle or brother who is called *eni mbumba* or *mwinimbumba, owner of the mbumba* in Dedza and is *'ambuye"* in Mulanje.

Children belong to the wife and the uncles are in control, the husband's role is largely procreational. In case of divorce or upon death of the wife the husband returns to his home village, leaving the house and the children. Polygamy is practised to some extent but the women stay in their respective villages

A man may take his wife to his home village under special circumstances. This practice is called *chitengwa* in Dedza and *ulowoka* in Mulanje. Before he takes the wife he is supposed to inform the chiefs of both villages in case of illness or death.

Implications of the Marriage Systems

Patrilineal system

Case study: Mrs. Chirwa is in her 30s; she has been married for nine years. She does not have children and that seems to have been a major issue in her marriage. Her parents died a while back and her only direct relative alive is her grandmother. She lives in her husband's home. She works on the tobacco fields and plants food crops. However, the husband controls all the proceeds. The tobacco permit is in his name even though she works on the farm on her own. She has since last year lived all by herself as her husband moved out and is living at his second wife's parent's home (something that is out of the norm in this patrilineal belt).

Mrs. Chirwa's husband had brought home a second wife two years ago. The two wives used to live in the same house, each with her own bedroom. A little over a year ago, the second wife decided she wanted to go and live at her parents' home. The husband agreed and followed her. When they moved, they took with them all household property and furniture including items (such as a bicycle) that Mrs. Chirwa had bought using her own money. Mrs. Chirwa continues to work on her husband's farm. He provides her with fertilizer otherwise she does all the work on her own. The man only comes during harvest time to supervise tobacco grading, bailing and have it sent to tobacco auction floors. For that and the ownership of land, the money goes into his bank account. When asked how she feels about it, Mrs. Chirwa says that she is not pleased but there is nothing she can do about it since it is his land and his home.

Mrs. Chirwa's co-wife delivered a baby last year; she thus has more control over the man and more status within the household. Mrs. Chirwa has tried to conceive to no avail – she wears beads around her waist – a sign of femininity and sexuality to enhance her beauty and her fertility. However, without the man being available for sex, her chances of conceiving are dimi-nished. Currently, Mrs. Chirwa reports that there is no sexual contact bet-ween them; the man only comes to her home to process the tobacco in the morning and leaves late in the afternoon after being given lunch and water to bathe. On our last visit in the village, Mrs. Chirwa asked her husband to take maize to the grinding mill on the bicycle. When the co-wife heard about it, she came to where we (all the women in the focus group discussion) were sitting but did not join our discussion, apparently she had wanted to check if

Mrs. Chirwa was the one who had sent the man on an errand.

Mrs. Chirwa's first five years of marriage were characterized by domestic violence. Initially, the man used to beat her up until when she decided to fight back. Whenever they fought and the man seemed to be losing, he resorted to biting her: she has three marks/scars on the face from his biting. She narrated that during one fighting incident; she was badly hurt bleeding through her nose and mouth. The man and his relatives simply kept her in the house until somebody from her home village heard about it and came to see her. This person than informed some of her extended family members who came and only then took her to the hospital. Having lost her parents and other economically able relatives, Mrs. Chirwa has no way of returning to her parent's village (her home) since there is nobody to return the cattle that her husband paid as *lobola* for her marriage, which is expected if she goes back. Her grandmother is too old and too poor to help. She is thus in a bind; yet an illustration of the nkhanza that women in her area are exposed to.

During the ongoing focus group discussion with the women, the issue of re-marriage was then discussed.

There was another woman who had been married whose husband took on a second wife. She (the first wife) had had three children with him. Tensions and fights in the home resulted in their divorce. The woman has since re-married and she is now a second wife. This prompted some discussion among the women as some felt that they would never do such a thing since it was the same polygyny that led to divorce: if a second wife caused problems in their marriage, why would they in turn want to be a second wife?

Because the men pay *lobola* to the wife's parents, they have the feeling that they have 'bought' the women and some tend to mistreat them especially if they are not producing any children. The man's family expects the woman to produce heirs to the property of the father or heirs to chieftaincy if the lineage is in their family. The same children are also labour force for the gardens and the fields.

Mothers-in-law tend to be very powerful and have the power to tell their son to divorce his wife if they are not happy with their daughter-in-law. Most daughters-in-law are mistreated by their in laws. Many lamented that they are treated as slaves. They have no say and they have no one to turn to since the village is not their home, as such *"timayankhulira pa mtondo" "we pour out our grievances through songs as we pound"*. According to a report on Women's Property and Inheritance Rights in Malawi by Ngwira et al (2002), the *lobola* is paid to legitimize the marriage and is used as a bond. It signifies that the woman surrenders her rights to ownership of property and children and in turn empowers the man as the sole owner and distributor of property. As such the women do not inherit anything when the husband dies or if they divorce. Another implication is that the women are not encouraged to get any support from their relatives because doing so is like undermining their husband's authority. If they get something from their relatives they are called "prostitutes".

The following quotes summarize the women's feeling about the patrilineal system: *"we are trapped"*, *"we envy our friends from the centre and the south"*.

Matrilineal system

Because the men live in the wife's village, they have less power as compared to the men in patrilineal systems. The husband may have authority over certain issues in his family. In fact, he has little say over matters affecting his own family since it is the uncle, the *mwinimbumba,* who plays a crucial role in decision making regarding issues of education, marriage, etc. Further, the women have some leeway because they are in their own village and they can challenge decisions made by the husband. Some are empowered to an extent that if they are fed up with a man's misbehaviour they can chase him away. Women in matrilineal areas (Dedza and Mulanje) preferred this system because when the marriage is over, at least they are left with the house and the children since they belong to her and the woman clan. For chitengwa or ulooka, most women did not like these marriage practices unless the man buys some land somewhere far from his village to settle with his family.

However, although women in the matrilineal societies occupy a central position in the social structure, it does not necessarily mean that they hold real power. It is still men, mostly the uncle, then the brother and to a lesser extent the husband, who exercise real power and authority over the family (Chirwa et al 1998, Saur 1991).

Perception of Nkhanza

Case study: Mrs. Banda, divorced woman with three daughters, matrilineal system, Chewa. Mrs. Banda is now a single mother with three daughters. Besides the hardship with her husband, who had abused her inflicting all forms of *Nkhanza* and then left her, and the hunger and starvation she had suffered in 2002, she informed us about a different form of violence perpetuated by women on women.

Mrs. Banda explained that her mother had beaten her when she was in labour, giving birth. The reason given was, that she was not allowed to cry out, she had to. repress her pain. So she was hurt because she was not able to conceal the pain caused by being in labour. This was a rather traumatic experience for her.

Although it is the cultural pattern in Chewa society that pain should not be shown in public like crying out when you are in labour, it is still considered *nkhanza* if your own mother forces you to abide by this pattern by beating you.

According to our interview partners, nurses in hospitals are behaving in a similar way. They reported that in a particular hospital different patterns of physical punishment and fiscal charges were applied to patients who did show their pain.

So, in Mrs. Banda's case she went from an abusive relationship with her mother to an abusive relationship with her husband. It illustrates the fact that women are subjugated to violence from all those who have authority over them. In their early lives to both parents and other family members, then in adult live to husbands and even still their own mother and most probably aunties too. One could conclude that the husband is 'replacing' the seniors of her family as the person who can abuse the wife in a way she has already grown to accept/expect by those above her.

Mrs. Banda developed an enormous fear that the – then already remarried – husband might come back to her village to beat her. This had happened in the past – and now the fear of it had become overwhelming, something that lurked over her like a grey cloud – always.

Mrs. Banda did not want to talk to us on the second day. She tried to hide from us when we walked past her place to another interviewee's house, as if we 'were after her' so to speak. We literally saw her running away when she had glimpsed us. The day before she had told us that she was going to her brother's house in another village, this being the reason for not wanting to continue the interview. When I then saw that she was hiding from us – since she had obviously not left for her brother's village – I thought she was re-enacting the fear from her husband – once a very intimate person now an enemy. Similarly she had also told us most intimate things and seemed then to conclude that we are now 'after her'. She had after all spoken negatively about her mother and her husband; that might have created anxiety, perhaps guilt. We asked another interviewee to please inform her, that it is absolutely and entirely up to her, whether she talks to us or not. And also, if she wanted to continue the next day, we would be very happy to talk to her again – if not we would be very understanding and she need not be afraid, embarrassed or anything. The next day she received us with a heartfelt welcome and would have loved to continue the interview for hours – which we sadly were not in a position to do. She described in depth again the volatile relationship with her husband and how glad she was to be out of it. She resented that he did not pay or support her in anyway, but made clear that she would rather struggle only being supported by her brother rather than be with her husband. She clearly prayed that he would stay away from the village.

The way Mrs. Banda described the power of her husband and the fear that it invoked in her, corresponds with the behaviour of battered women throughout the world who, as research has shown, also tend to see their ex-partners, the perpetrators, more much as powerful than they are in reality. They are often afraid that not even several policemen could restrain the husband in court so that they would still be able to attack them. Mrs. Banda had experienced that neighbours and family could not protect her from him, so the fear became an almost all-consuming feeling.

A male member of the village community though, referred to Mrs. Banda's case by saying that she had not wanted to work in the fields and therefore deserved the misfortune she suffered. This corresponds with a universal theme that women are accused of: It is often said that the abuse is due to their own fault after all, since they behaved so 'provocatively' for example. It corresponds to our findings that the so-called 'educational beat-ing' was seen as an accepted method to treat a woman – by men and women a like.

The fear for women like Mrs. Banda, of being persecuted by the former violent partner till they are killed corresponds with findings worldwide, since this is often the case and was confirmed in our study by the cases from Chief Kukada for example. On the other hand it shows battered women's necessarily distorted view of men or their battering partner that makes it so hard for them to leave in the first place. They do not fight back or leave because they are afraid of being killed if they do so.

Likewise this case shows that mothers seem to have lifelong authority to apply physical violence to their daughters.

Nkhanza inflicted by women on women was reconfirmed by data we got from a hospital where penalties were issued according to the patient's behaviour, i.e. if pain was uttered in a noise making way one was exposed to a physical punishment and fiscal charge.

Both examples show that the authorities, be they in the family or else-where, determine what pain has to be endured without being shown and to reprimand people who cannot help to do so.

It shows that violence is accepted yet again – and the person who questions is violated even more, is added to injury.

Women's Perception of Violence/Nkhanza

This subsection discusses what women perceived as violence (Nkhanza). The study evaluated the difference between ideal and reality by asking questions on who a real woman is, what causes conflicts, their general perception of violence, the type of violence women perpetrate against fellow women and the violence women perpetrate against men. The women also talked about the disadvantages of patrilocal residence.

Focus group discussion of women with Chief Nyamaduna and Linda Semu. Women demonstrate through dancing how they are portrayed in songs. Photo: Maria Saur

A 'Real' (Ideal) Woman

Characteristics of a real woman can be grouped into four main categories: personality traits, relationship with her husband, household responsibilities, sexual attributes and fertility. (Although we asked for the characteristics of a real/normal woman we were rather presented with the perception of an 'ideal' woman.)

Personality traits

"She should be well mannered."

"She should be God-fearing."

"She should be trustworthy."

"She should not be a gossiper."

Interpersonal relationship with her husband

"She should not be shy with her husband; should be able to undress in front of her husband and when you bath together she should be able to bath her husband, even his private parts."

"She should love her husband."

Sexual attributes

"She should positively assist her husband when having sex; should be able to wriggle her waist to satisfy his sexual needs otherwise he will go for other women."

"She should have labia minora like a pig's balls which a man should play with during foreplay" (only in the southern region).

Household responsibilities

"She should be able to do household chores such as sweeping, cooking, washing dishes."

"She should be able to warmly welcome visitors from her husband's side and cook for them."

"She should be able to take care of her husband when he is sick."

Fertility

"She should be able to bear children; if she can't have children they look for traditional medicine and if there is still no improvement, the man leaves her for another woman who can give him children."

Women's perception of Violence/Nkhanza

There was a general consensus amongst the women in the three study districts that there are two types of wife beating.

Educational beating

This is the type of beating where the man slaps the woman or uses a stick. This educational beating is acceptable in their eyes because the man is trying to tell her to change her behaviour. As one woman put it during one focus group discussion *"When the man slaps you it means he loves you. He does not want you to go back to your village but that you should just change your behaviour, it could be that he has tried several times but you did not listen".* It is worth noting that being beaten by the man after having done something "wrong" is not considered nkhanza. In that case the violent person is the woman.

Violent beating

This beating is seen as not acceptable as the man leaves the woman with injuries such as broken ribs and there is loss of blood. Usually such cases go to the chief or to the police.

Beating without any apparent reason

This was said to be the case when the men are drunk. At their drinking places they would pick up a quarrel with someone and would project the anger on the wife and act it out on her. Actually one lady in Dedza said, "A *man has a heart like a baby's, when he quarrels with his friends at a beer drinking place he would come and beat you at home".*

Having sex with your wife too frequently

Women said that some men do not give their women a break from conjugating; the only time they can rest is when they are menstruating. Some said that even in the late pregnancy some men would demand sex until the day when she goes to deliver. This was seen as *nkhanza.*

Not taking care of the family

One of the major responsibilities of the man is to take care of his family i.e. buying food, clothing for the wife and the children. If he does not do these things then he is considered inflicting *nkhanza.*

Refusing to have sex with the wife

According to the women, this is the most serious form of *nkhanza.* As they told us, marriage is all about sex. If the man says no to her sexual advances then he has offended her and that issue can be taken to the *ankhoswe.* The women actually said "it *married me because of that. Me too I want to have it".* Although this was a general perception amongst women, women in Rumphi especially those in polygamous marriages, cherish these moments with their husbands particularly, as they see them as the only times when they are really appreciated. It also seems that it is the only time they have access to their husbands in terms of being heard and listened to.

Being stingy

Women told us that some men do not allow their wives to cook anything when they have gone somewhere. Some men actually leave marks in maize flour baskets. And, as stated earlier, it was also discovered that a chicken is a most valuable asset and a woman can not just decide on her own to prepare a one even if it's hers. A certain woman lamented "...*you can not slaughter even your own chicken because you did not raise it at your own home*". This is just echoing the fact that women have no voice especially when it comes to decision making and also that they are not regarded as part of the family especially when *lobola* has been paid – in patrilocal and lineal families.

Not allowing the wife to have time to chat with her friends.

Some men erect boundaries which the women cannot pass.

Forced sex

Forcing the wife to have sex with the partner when she is not ready and when she does not feel like having sex. This issue was brought by women in Mulanje. Most women in Mulanje have had exposure to human rights and are aware of their rights so it is considered rape and unlawful now. Women from the other districts also clearly felt that being forced to have sex is not right but do not call it rape yet.

Marrying another woman without informing the first wife

In areas where polygamy is common especially in Rumphi this was seen as a form of nkhanza. Men marry second or third wives during the tobacco-selling period when they have money. They can just meet someone at the market and bring her home. Under normal circumstances, the man is supposed to inform his wife when he wants to marry another woman. This does not mean that the man is asking for the wife's approval, he can still bring another woman home without the wife's consent. Telling her is just a matter of courtesy. Yet if the wife is barren she can actually tell the husband to marry another woman.

Unequal division of love to the co-wives

When the man has more than one wife he should love the women equally. This means to spend the same number of days at each one's house or bedroom, buy the same food, clothes etc. If he does not fulfil his obligations then there is tension between the women.

Nkhanza Perpetrated by Women on Women

This section discusses the types of nkhanza women perpetrate on fellow women. These can be grouped into broad categories: violence between women in a polygamous marriage, a friend sleeping with one's husband, jealousy, stinginess.

Issues in polygamous marriage

Co-wives in a polygamous marriage often do not like each other, especially if the man did not inform the first wife about marrying a co-wife. Unlike in matrilineal systems where the women live in their respective villages, in patrilineal areas such as Rumphi the women live within the same compound this breeds a lot of tension among the women and they do a lot of things to outdo each other; for example:

Witchcraft

"Every woman wants a man for herself, if he marries another woman you have to find charms so that he should not want her, or she should go mad or she should just go back to her village."

"When your co-wife is pregnant you find charms so that she should miscarry."

Fighting

"Co wives fight a lot mainly because of jealousy. The women give each other turns to have the man at their home; for example a man is supposed to stay for a week at one wife's place, if he does not go to the other it causes conflicts. In Dedza there was a case where the first wife hacked the second wife because the man had spent more days than they agreed."

"When a man finds another woman you beat her because she is a source of conflicts in your marriage, after all you can't fight your husband so you have to beat her up."

"I'd kill her and beat him up"

Not taking care of the co-wife's children

It was often reported that some women refuse to share food and beat their co-wife's children.

A woman sleeping with her friend's husband.

In all the study areas this was mentioned as the most common and the most serious forms of nkhanza among women.

> "Women go out with another woman's husband and laugh at her that 'we do share whatever your man has'.

Fighting

Women fight at water boreholes and break each others' pails because some of them try to jump queues. This happens especially where the boreholes are not enough for the whole village and water is a problem.

Gossip

The study also established that women fight because of gossip. It was said that the root causes are the husbands. When he meets one woman and says bad things about the other, the first will publicize it.

Stinginess

Refusing to share food, salt, household items such as mortar and pestle, mats, etc

Jealousy outside marriage

> "When you are unmarried and doing well, people think of you as a prostitute."
>
> "Being jealous of you because you are better off than them."

Nkhanza Perpetrated by Women on Men

This section discusses the kinds of nkhanza women perpetrate on men according to what the women themselves said. The broad categories include: sexuality, interpersonal relationship with husbands, being irresponsible as a woman and a wife, chasing away the husband after divorce.

Sexuality issues

"Refusing to have sex with your husband when you have quarrelled or when you are upset with him is a very serious punishment."

"Sleeping with another woman's husband."

Interpersonal relationships with husbands

"Being disrespectful to your husband i.e. answering back rudely."

"Calling your husband by using one of your children's names for example 'John's father' instead of using his clan name for instance 'Ambewe' or 'Aphiri'."

"Not warmly welcoming your husband when he is back from wherever he went."

"Locking your husband out when he is coming from his drinking spree".

"Soaking your husband's clothes so that he should not go anywhere, especially drinking."

"Pouring boiling water over him when you have had enough."

Being irresponsible as a woman and as a wife

"Not preparing food for your husband or warming food when he comes home late."

"Not doing his laundry"

"Not giving him bath water when the couple has quarrelled or when the man is coming back from drinking."

"Spending your time gambling when you haven't finished your household chores."

"Spending your time chatting with friends without taking care of your husband".

Chasing the men away after divorce/death

This was common in Dedza and Mulanje districts where the men reside in the wife's village. It was mentioned that after divorce or when the wife dies the man is told to go back to his village. Normally, they do not have anything at their home because all their investment is done at the woman's place, which he regards as his home.

Violence experienced by women as a result of patrilocal residence

Women in Rumphi gave their analysis of violence as a result of living with a man in his village as the matrimonial home. They said that as a result of men paying *lobola* for them, some men tend to mistreat their wives. The situation is even worse when the woman's relatives are dead, especially those that received the *lobola,* because there is no one to return the bride wealth, if she were to go back. The woman is victimized by her in-laws, she is expected to work long hours looking after her own home as well as her parents-in-law.

"The first week you are treated well but afterwards you become their slave."

"The problem is that you actually follow the man, so we just have to accept the situation because we want the marriage to work"

"When your relatives are dead the paternal relatives mistreat you because they know that there is no one who will give back lobola."

Case Study: Mrs. Phiri, unmarried, youngest female interviewee, from Ngoni Village.

Mrs. Phiri very early had bad experiences with physical violence perpetrated by a tutor/class-mate who had helped her to catch up in school after she had long been absent due to a recurring illness.

The young man would wait for her after school and beat her if she was seen even chatting with other people. She could neither understand nor hardly endure what was going on for quite a while. Then she became sick. Due to the illness her feet and legs were swelling up so badly that she could not walk anymore and could therefore not go to school. When she finally recovered and went back to school the harassment and beating continued. First her brother then her father intervened and told the young man to stay away from the girl. The beating eventually stopped.

Despite all the hardship and obstacles encountered – the sickness with swollen feet/legs often recurred – Mrs. Phiri was very enthusiastic about her education and persevered to do the MSCE/O'Level.

Then she had to face up to the next obstacle – the financial one. Her family couldn't possibly pay for her education so she tried to find other supporters. One person in Canada who funded her cousin did not want to fund her too and told her so in a rather insulting way, i.e. "how dare you ask me". Mrs. Phiri was very hurt but not discouraged. She found a job in a doctor's private practice where again due to financial reasons she was eventually made redundant.

She is still very keen to do more training and to find a proper job, to be able to help her ageing parents and her sister who is a single mother.

The next job she did not get because she refused to sleep with the prospective employer who made that a condition.

Since she could not find a job so far she has resigned herself to getting married. She has made it part of her marriage negotiations that she should be allowed to go for more training and education – but this request has been unsuccessful as yet. Instead she was successful in demanding that her future husband and herself do go for an HIV/Aids test in the capital before the wedding, which they did!

As part of the wedding arrangements the future husband is in the process of building a house for her in her parents' compound. She still hopes that in the long run the husband will help her to find a job and get further education, and will be a gentle and loving person who would rather live by the new pop song –"Don't beat her she is so beautiful" than by the traditional wedding song "Beating is the oil of marriage".

Men's Perceptions of Gender-Based Violence

In discerning men's perceptions of gender-based violence, the study evaluated the discrepancy between the ideal and reality by asking questions on: who a real man is, what causes conflict, the type of violence that men perpetrate on fellow men and what the men perpetrate on women. The men in matrilineal villages also narrated the negative aspects of matrilocal residence. Here again as in the women's case the men portrayed rather an 'ideal man'.

A 'real' (ideal) Man

Characteristics of a real man fall into four categories: fertility, ability to provide for one's family, admirable characteristics and signs of material well-being.

Fertility

> "A real man should be able to get it up and bear children, and not be an impotent or infertile man. Actually, that is the core of manhood."

> "When a man says: 'I am a man', what he means is that he can bear children and he has several wives."

Ability to provide for the family

"He should be hardworking, for example, he should be able to construct a house, a granary and a rubbish pit. That way, the woman surrenders her body to you".

"He should be a good farmer: there should be adequate food in the home, as well as livestock."

"He should be able to provide food, clothing, soap, salt and other necessities in the home."

Admirable characteristics

"He should be nice."

"He should not beat up his wife."

"He should be willing to share what he has: he should not be stingy."

"He should be able to warmly welcome visitors."

"He should be peace-loving."

Signs of material well being

"His home is well provided for: they have all their needs."

"He and his family should be well dressed."

"He should have a bicycle."

"Gets along with friends, relatives, neighbours and other people."

Causes of conflict

Despite the idealized view of the real man presented above, research participants acknowledged that the reality is that there are conflicts and misunderstandings between women and men in families, and also amongst men in their day-to-day interaction. Causes of conflicts and misunderstandings fall under the three broad categories of: communication, the personal relationship between a couple, and behaviour related issues.

Communication

"Failure to discern what your spouse likes or dislikes. This is compounded by the fact that most couples do not sit down to tell each other in advance what they like or dislike."

The personal relationship between the couple

"When a spouse refuses to have sex with her/his partner."

"When the man has sex with other women."

"Jealousy that comes about when a spouse is talking to a member of the opposite sex and you are not comfortable with the way they are relating to each other."

Behaviour-related issues

"Nagging your spouse."

"Stealing money or other household items and selling them in order to get money for beer drinking."

"Being rude."

"Wanting things you cannot afford and comparing your family status to what is happening in other families."

"Not wanting to share what you have with your family."

"Being lazy."

"Getting back home late from a drinking spree."

"A woman using magic/love portions so that she can control her husband."

Nkhanza Perpetrated by Men on Men

While physical violence was acknowledged as a problem, the men indicated that most of the violence has to do with the kinds of inter-personal relationships they have with one another in their everyday interaction. The broad categories of violence mentioned during the study were: a friend going out with one's wife; fighting; not wanting to share what one has; jealousy; leadership issues; looking down upon others, grabbing land from someone, and stealing.

A friend having sex with your wife

This was viewed as the most serious form of nkhanza and was mentioned in all the six villages where data was collected.

"A friend who sleeps with your wife is as good as the two of them killing you: the people that you trust and rely on are your friend and your wife so

if the two of them go behind your back and have sex, it means they don't love you."
"Some men actually buy beer for you so that you get drunk and they sneak out and go to your house to have sex with your wife."

Fighting

"This usually occurs when there is a communication breakdown. Sometimes, men fight after drinking beer because they compete against each other over something."

Not giving assistance to others

"Men will at times not share their money with a fellow man who is suffering. Yet the same man will be glad to give money to a woman."
"Not wanting to share your beer with other men when you go drinking. In some cases, some men partake in the beer that others buy and yet they do not reciprocate."
"Not turning up to assist a man who has a major job to be done such as constructing a house."

Jealousy

"Being jealous of a fellow man because he is better off."
"Some men go to the extent of looking for charms to bewitch the other person. Usually, the charms are expensive so some men might commit a whole year's income from their tobacco for buying the charm"."

Leadership issues

"Some individuals, particularly chiefs are like dictators: they do not want to listen to other views. Rather, they expect people to just follow their wishes."
"Some men deliberately make life difficult for those who have positions of authority for example, by not turning up for meetings or not contributing to development work."
"Some men simply like to disturb the peace in villages."
"Choosing not to pay people after they have done piece work for you."

Looking down upon others

"Lack of respect for one another"

"Undermining other men because you are materially better off than they are."

"Embarrassing a man that you have helped by telling other people about it or mentioning about the assistance you have given him in a condescending manner in public."

Theft

"Stealing from other people's homes and gardens."

Land issues

Grabbing a piece of land from someone. This was considered quite a serious act of violence in view of people's dependence on subsistence farming. This occurs within families where people who are related have conflicting claims over land or in cases where there are boundary disputes.

Nkhanza Perpetrated by Men on Women

Just like the nkhanza that men perpetrate on fellow men, the one perpetrated on women is not only physical but is related to the inter-personal relationships between both sexes in their daily interaction. The broad categories of nkhanza mentioned during the study were: fighting, stinginess, sexuality issues, failure to live up to responsibilities and behaviour-related issues.

"Bearing in mind that there is an accepted form of wife beating, men in all villages deplored cases where the man beats up the wife without a valid reason or for no specific reason."

Stinginess

"Not giving your wife money and food"

"Giving orders to your wife not to prepare meals if you are not at home. Some can go to the extent of putting marks on the maize flour so that they will know if the wife prepared lunch in their absence. Some go to the extent of writing UP/Ukatapa Upita (if you take out some to the flour that will be the end of the marriage.)"

"Some men check in the relish pot to see how much of the meat is left before they leave the house."

"If there is meat, sugar, soap and other things, the wife is not allowed to use them without seeking permission form the husband."

"Using herbs e.g. *gondolosi* to enhance performance since it is painful for the woman." (practised in the South)

Sexuality issues

"Refusing to have sex with your wife yet that is the reason behind getting married: A person can get nsima and fish from their parent's home and other relatives but they need to have sex with their spouses."

"Sexually neglecting one wife and focusing on the other one if you are polygamously married."

"Forcing your wife to have sex with you when she is tired, sick or upset."

"Demanding sex throughout the night without giving your wife time to rest."

"Going out with other women."

"Taking on another wife without informing your wife."

"Infecting your wife with sexually transmitted infections."

Failure to live up to one's responsibilities as a man

"Alcoholism."

"Not sharing with your wife money realized from sales of agricultural produce. Some men sell agricultural produce and spend the money on beer."

"Spending the night at a drinking place."

"Stealing your wife's housekeeping money and using it to buy beer."

"Not providing for the wife and family."

"Forcing your wife to have too many children."

"Not helping your wife with household chores when she is pregnant."

"Not escorting your wife to the hospital when a child is sick."

"Denying responsibility for a pregnancy."

Behaviour-related violence

"Some men like to shout at the top of their voice when they are coming back from a drinking spree. In matrilineal areas, such men take advantage of the fact that they are drunk to settle scores with the wife and her relatives."

"Curtailing a woman' freedoms by stopping her from going to some places, preventing her from forming friendships with other people and not allowing her to buy the things that she wants."

Violence experienced by men as a result of matrilocal residence

Men in Dedza and Mulanje pointed out that there is some violence that is perpetrated against them because of the *chikamwini* system. Their analysis of their situation was based on the word *mkamwini* itself which means "it (he) belongs to someone else thus – somebody's child only here for marriage." The men generally felt that they are always under scrutiny from the parents' in laws and the wife's other relatives. In cases where their wives had several sisters all of whom were married, they expressed that there tended to be competition amongst the men in terms of whose family is doing better materially. The parents in law also tend to favour one son in law instead of treating all the sons-in-law equally. Specifically, violence experienced under *chikamwini* is in the broad categories of: lack of control over offspring; not being treated well and being viewed as an outsider irrespective of time spent in the village. Thus they felt they lack security in marriage and old age.

Men's perceptions of the violence that they experience because of the chikamwini *system*

"You raise a child jointly with your wife but once the child is grown, the maternal uncle takes charge and the child supports him more than s/he supports the father."

"We are told that our only job is to bear children".

"When a child finds parents in a fight, the child sides with the mother and beats up the father."

"We are told to go back to our homes when we get old."

"Upon the death of your wife, you are expected to go back to your village and leave behind the children."

"If you are not living up to expectations or if you are abusive to your wife, her family will chase you away."

"Mmuniko" (light) whereby they will light some long grasses and use them to illuminate and show you where you came from in case you have forgotten or they can take a string to your home and give it to your relatives and ask them to use it to tie you up so that you can go back to your home."

Focus group discussion Men with chief Mung'anya and Stella Ndau. Photo: M. Saur

Children's Perception of Violence

This section discusses the children's perception of violence. The study showed that whatever the children reported confirmed what the parents had said violence is, and also what the parents are doing. For example their definitions of violence/Nkhanza were also to do with inter-personal relationships. Overall, the children – like their parents – said that violence is being stingy i.e. not sharing food, beating without any offence, killing without any reason, being mistreated by the parents and others.

Below is a summary of what the children said about which kind of nkhanza was perpetrated by the parents on them as children.

Violence perpetrated by parents on children

Beating children

The children said that parents, especially mothers, beat them when they have had a fight with their fathers. Since they feel helpless to fight back the fathers, the mothers most likely act it out on the children. Most children were of the view that parents have a right to beat them because they are

Focus Group Discussion Children; Girls' group in Kapesi. Photo: Maria Saur

Children and they need guidance to grow up with good manners. One girl said *"a child can not just grow up without being beaten; it should be beaten so that he should not repeat the same mistakes"*. Much as they said that it is all right for parents to beat them, they did not like the fact that they were beaten during meal times so that they could not eat the food. They also said that because they are young and innocent, sometimes they do not realize that they have made a mistake and they need proper guidance rather than being beaten!

Not being given food

When they have made a mistake they are not given food as a punishment. This was seen as one of the most serious forms of nkhanza which parents perpetrate on their children.

Not being given proper assistance with school needs

Some parents do not provide necessities such as notebooks, pencils and pens for school needs.

Absenteeism

Parents absent their children from school in order to help them with household chores such as looking after their siblings, sending them to the maize-mill, to the garden, to draw water, etc. Additionally, some children complained that their parents send them on too many errands such that they do not find time to study or to do their homework, let alone to play with their friends.

Violence perpetrated by children on parents

Shouting obscenities

Children said that they don't do this out of the blue, they just follow suit what the parents themselves do; *"We the children copy whatever our parents do to be the norm, actually it's them who start swearing at us"*. They also alleged that they shout at their parents, for example, when they come home drunk and especially when they do not provide for the family, spending the money on beer instead.

Refusing to do household chores

Some children said that occasionally they refuse, for example, going to the maize mill, drawing water, or going to the garden because those places are far away from their home. From time to time they have to go when they are tired or haven't had any food.

Beating the parents

The feeling was that it was wrong to be beating each other especially one's own parents, but again they said that they just follow their parents' example of fighting. They said that the parents fight when they have disagreements such as: when either of them does not go to the garden/field, when the mother refuses to sleep with her husband or when they are drunk. In Mulanje and Dedza, the children said that when their parents fight they take sides with their mother and beat the father because they can't beat their mother who breastfed them; and if they beat her who would cook food for them. This situation of children taking sides with their mothers and beating their fathers echoes the situation of men in matrilineal systems where they do not have effective authority and power over their own children.

"Parents should stop drinking beer excessively because when they are drunk they behave like mad people: they swear, they fight. We do not have peace in our homes and we run away to our grandparents or uncles."

"On Thursdays you can't like our village, our village is noisy while our friends' are very quiet and peaceful."

"People puke all over the roads."

Things they would like to change in their lives

During the discussions the children were able to talk freely about the things they would want to see changed for the better in their lives. Among the things mentioned were that parents, especially in Dedza where both men and women drink, should stop drinking excessively because when they are drunk they behave like mad: they shout obscenities at their own children, they fight, the mothers do not cook for the children and the young ones end up confused, and psychologically tortured. The children are made to mature when they are very young and are taking up big responsibilities of taking care of siblings. As a result most of them are dropping out of school.

Secondly, they were of the view that both parents and the youth should stop indulging in extra marital and premarital malpractices respectively, because most people in their villages are dying of HIV/AIDS. Consequently, there are many orphans in the villages. Regarding these orphans, they said they know many of them who are being mistreated by their relatives. One boy actually said that the government should start orphanages in their villages, as there are just so many orphans. Furthermore, they also said that they would be glad if more schools and boreholes were built in the villages. For some children in one of the villages in Mulanje the nearest school is an hour away and they only have one borehole such that most of them go to shower at the river because they cannot handle the queues in the morning, otherwise they would be late for school.

In addition, they said that they would be happier if teachers stopped giving corporal and heavy punishments to pupils as well as impregnating schoolgirls.

On their experiences during the hunger period, most of them narrated that they did not have enough food and used to rely on tubers, okra soup and vegetables. Most of them dropped out of school and would go to fetch firewood for sale and buy some *"walkman"*. They remembered vividly how people used to steal from other people's gardens and how individuals died after being beaten when found stealing from hunger.

Most of the villagers would not have enough food to last them this year because according to the children: *"People did not have fertilizer; their gardens are not big enough to produce more food. Even though they received the starter pack, some of them do sell it and use the money for something else."*

The following quotation from one of the girls during the focus group discussions summarizes the depth of sorrow the children have due to their plight and the hunger they experienced.

"Kukhosi kwanga kwatseka ndipo sizingatulukenso"-
"My throat is strangled with sorrow and I can speak no more".

Focus group discussion with children and research assistant Emmie Kumbikano.
They are peeling maize grain of the stalk which will then be used as fuel.
Photo: Maria Saur

Case Study: Structural Violence, Mr. Sobo, 23, trying to bring up 7 siblings alone, Tumbuka Village

Mr. Sobo, a young man, now ca. 23 years old (he has lost track of his age), used to enjoy going to school and had high ambitions to pursue a career, he wanted to become a medical doctor. His aspirations were put to an abrupt end when both his parents died of AIDS. He was about 15 years old then and was left with 7 siblings the youngest a little baby. He had to look after his bothers and one sister. There was no time left to go to school nor was there money to pay any school fees. He tried to till the land with the help of his siblings but they did not harvest enough to feed them all, even though school had been abandoned by all of them to be able to do so. He decided to move to a tobacco estate in the hope of finding work for him and the elder brothers and schooling for the others. This failed since they were abused to such an extend that Mr. Sobo thought it better to move back to their home village. The little land they own, is now let to other framers and he and his brothers work as piece-workers on other people's land to get a 'cash income'.

None of the siblings could really pursue school for the sheer struggle of survival, which is Mr. Sobo's biggest concern. He dearly hopes that one day there will be help, so that they can go to school.

He had meanwhile married in the hope, that with the help of his new wife they could cope better. But the wife and their first child both died in childbirth. So he was left alone again and now feels completely abandoned and heartbroken.

The chief's family does help him 'with salt' meaning 'little things,' but otherwise he has not received any support at all. Mr. Sobo did not know about the Community Welfare Officer as a person who could be addressed in cases like his. Instead he helps an elderly lady, who is an AIDS orphan herself – all her children have recently passed away. The brothers borrow a bike on a regular basis from a neighbour to fetch water for themselves and the lone lady. This is the only way to get water, since men are not expected to carry it on their heads.

The sister has meanwhile married and is living elsewhere.

Mr. Sobo feels that the system has failed him – a very promising student once – and all his siblings totally. His greatest wish is that his brothers could go back to school to at least get a basic education instead of working in the fields to try and make ends meet – which they still do not even manage.

We visited Mr. Sobo's house in the fairly well to do tobacco growing environment. He and his brothers, all un-typically thin for the region and the season, are living in the poorest of conditions. One brother has now developed a mental illness.

Structural Issues and Processes

This section reviews the dispute resolution structure that is followed in the villages. This process was conducted on two levels: the primary system and the formal structures of justice. In addition, people's assessment of the structures of justice is presented. Overall, the study has found that people in the villages trust and rely upon the local traditional systems and see them as playing a useful role in supplying access to justice. These systems are proximate, flexible and faster in responding to problems as they arise. The formal system is viewed as being alien, unreliable and more of a service for the urban elite. In particular, many do not understand the procedures followed and dislike the lack of participatory processes in reaching decisions. Problems of accessibility further compound the gap between the formal structures and people in the villages.

Primary System of Justice

Sources and causes of disputes vary. Generally, the following are some of the disputes resolved at the primary level: marriage disputes, paternity and pregnancy issues, witchcraft, theft of farm produce, land disputes, fights and alcohol induced disputes. In presenting the process involved in dispute resolution, emphasis will be placed on how marital disputes are resolved as this has implications on the acceptance of gender-based violence and on how it is best to be combated. There are several stages that are followed in the resolution of a marital dispute. The order is presented below:

Figure 1: Dispute Resolution Process

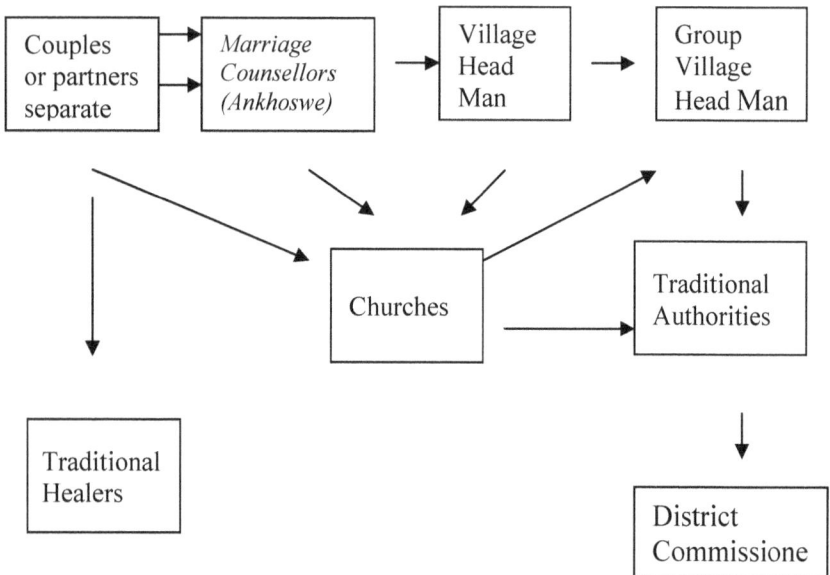

| Couples or partners separate | → → | *Marriage Counsellors (Ankhoswe)* | → | Village Head Man | → | Group Village Head Man |

Churches

Traditional Authorities

Traditional Healers

District Commissione

Marriage counsellors – ankhoswe

They are important in the recognition of a marriage in both matrilineal and patrilineal areas. The process through which the *ankhoswe* from the man and woman's families negotiate and cement the marriage is called *chinkhoswe*. A union without having undergone *chinkhoswe* is traditionally not considered as a marriage. In Rumphi, one's *nkhoswe* is always from the paternal side, it be an uncle, paternal aunt or any other male relative. In Dedza and Mulanje, the *nkhoswe* is usually from the maternal side, it can be an uncle (mother's brother) or one's older sibling. The ankhoswe's roles range from: facilitating the marriage process, being key in an individual's critical life events and playing an active role in solving day to day marital conflicts, especially involving sexual matters and/or in case of a divorce.

In facilitating the marriage, a spokesperson from one's side is chosen. (S)he is responsible for negotiating all arrangements associated with the marriage including *lobola* in the North. All problems that arise during the marriage are brought to the attention of this person initially. In turn, (s)he reports to an older *nkhoswe*.

Despite the differences between the matrilineal and patrilineal kinship structures, the roles of the *ankhoswe* are similar in the two systems.

In times of illness and/or death of either of the spouses or offspring, the *ankhoswe* must be informed, failure to do so results in the imposition of heavy fines. The *ankhoswe* are also responsible for resolving marital disputes such as:

> "Resolving fights that arise because of the husband's failure to provide for the family."
>
> "If the wife is lazy and does not maintain cleanliness in the home."
>
> "If the wife steals money from the husband's and/or if she takes household items and gives them to other people without consulting/ informing the husband."
>
> "If a man finds traditional medicine in the home of which he was not informed, he can take the issue to the ankhoswe on the grounds it might be a love potion that the wife intends to use on him."
>
> "If a couple fights, the issue is taken to the ankhoswe."

Sexual matters

In Dedza and Mulanje, the *ankhoswe* act as sex counsellors to the couple and all sexual matters arising are referred to them. In Rumphi, a man's aunt referred to as *ankhazi* does perform this role. In both cases, sexual matters brought to their attention are situations where:

Male complaints

When the wife refuses to have sex, the man can complain to the *ankhoswe*. *"After all that [sex] is the core of the marriage, if it is a matter of nsima and relish, one can get those from one's parents but not the sex.*

Female complaints

If a man is impotent or is not sexually performing up to standard, the wife can raise the issue with the ankhoswe for their assistance. She can just claim to them that *"there is nothing happening, I am sharing the bed with my brother, if not a fellow woman."* Similarly, if the man is demanding too much sex, the woman can also go and complain to the ankhoswe.

Divorce

Women in Dedza and Mulanje are able to initiate divorce whereas this is much harder for women in Rumphi because of *lobola*. Most women indicated that it becomes difficult for them to initiate divorce because if they do so, they are required to repay the *lobola* and in most cases, it would have by then been used up by their family either to enable a brother to acquire a wife or for other consumption needs. As such, many women are trapped in marriages that they would otherwise want to terminate:

> "We are slaves, we leave our homes to come and stay at the man's place, so we have to accommodate the man and make sure he does not divorce us."

> "Women in the North are in serious problems, our fellow women in the South are better off. Here we are slaves."

In Dedza and Mulanje, a woman can go to the *ankhoswe* to initiate divorce if she is fed up with the behaviour of the man; for example if he uses abusive language, is a drunkard, is 'fond of' beating her up for flimsy reasons or does not provide for the family. In such cases, the woman's *ankhoswe* will inform their counterpart from the man's side. The *nkhoswe* does not issue a divorce but rather takes the issue to the chief. It was emphasized during the study by different groups of women and men that the *ankhoswes'* role is to ensure as much as possible that the couple stays married.

This has implications on eradicating gender-based violence as in most cases the message from the *ankhoswe* is that one should persevere in marriage and that wife beating is the oil of the marriage. A concerted effort would have to be made to deliberately target the *ankhoswe* so that they are able to identify cases of gender-based violence and tackle them promptly in an adapted manner. As it is, most cases of gender-based violence go unreported and are accepted as the norm.

Village Head - Mfumu

Chiefs resolve a broad range of cases and are the main conduit through which people in rural areas access justice. The institution of chieftaincy in rural areas provides people with a sense of personal and collective safety, security for their property and a medium through which problems are resolved when they arise. The resolve cases related to marital problems, criminal matters and witchcraft. The following are cases that are brought to chiefs for resolution.

Marital disputes

Continuous marital problems, which the *ankhoswe* are not able to resolve, are brought to the chief for resolution. Those unions for which there was no *chinkhoswe* are dissolved at the chief's level. The duly recognized marriages are referred to the Traditional Authority for divorce. Marital dispute cases brought to the chief can be:

"Arguments between the couple which the ankhoswe have failed to resolve."

"If the man is too stingy and uses abusive language on the wife, her parents and other people."

"If a couple fights and the village gets to know about it, for example when the woman runs outside for help and a commotion ensues. In that case, the person who is in the wrong is charged a chicken for breach of peace."

"In matrilineal areas, if a man takes household items to his parents home."

"Arson: if a man burns down a house just because he is divorced from his wife and he has to go back to his home".

Criminal and other matters

"Fighting where blood has not been drawn."

"Disputes over land boundaries and entitlements."

"Cases of adultery where men are fighting over a woman."

"Failure to repay a loan – whether it's owed to an individual or was acquired through a group loan scheme."

"Paternity cases where a man is denying responsibility for a pregnancy."

"Accusations of witchcraft."

"Disputes arising at funerals especially where the gravediggers (adzukulu) either feel that they have been verbally abused by the family of the deceased or they have not been given adequate food by the family."

Group Village Head and the Church

The next stage in the hierarchy of dispute resolution is the group village head and/or the church. If a case is not resolved at this stage, then it is referred to the Traditional Authority for the final word. In cases of marital disputes, once the issue is brought to the village head and it remains unresolved, the head may recommend that the couple be counselled at their church/mosque if they are members of a faith community. However, most people feel that apart from the counselling that they may get, their faith communities are not very helpful as they are mostly reluctant to endorse a divorce. For example, some women who are members of the Catholic Church indicated that:

> "We cannot get a divorce. The priest would simply remind us that the marriage was sealed in church so if we want a divorce we should take up the matter with the Pope who would then nullify the marriage."

This is definitely a daunting task and intimidating to the women. In most cases, women are forced to stay in abusive marriages for fear of being excommunicated from the church should they decide to divorce. As an institution it was mentioned as one of the most reliable and accessible to people in villages during the study, *so it is important for the church to become more flexible as this has implications for the eradication of gender-based violence.*

Traditional Authority

The traditional authority (TA) is the highest in the traditional social organization and dispute resolution hierarchy. It is held in high esteem and awe. (In Mulanje, men kept referring to it as *"kumalata"* meaning modern structures that are found at the TA's court whose roof has iron sheets/*malata).* Marital disputes, criminal matters and accusations of witchcraft are brought to the TA's court as the final stage in the dispute resolution process. Usually, those that had a *chinkhoswe* marriage can get a divorce at the TA's court after the issue has gone through the various stages of dispute resolution presented above. In Rumphi, divorce is granted at the TA's court and it is determined if *lobola* is to be paid back to the man's family. In Dedza and Mulanje, divorce cases are held at the TAs court to ensure that the man does not abrogate his responsibility over his children. Before a divorce is granted, the court has to ensure that the man built a house in the woman's home and if there are any children, the man has to pay maintenance on a monthly basis through the court. Men in Kukada village in Mulanje had this to say about the TA's court:

> "Most of us are scared of the ruling and fines granted at the court. One might have gone through the ankhoswe's and the chief's resolution process where you adamantly indicated you no longer wanted to be married to your wife. However, when you get to the TA's court and if you happen to sit in on another couple's divorce hearing, the penalties are enough to make you change your mind. The TA might order the man to provide a 50 kilogram bag of maize and MK 1,000.00 every month. In that case, you just change your mind and you tell the court that she is my wife; I want to stay married to her."

The District Commissioner

As head of administration at the district level, the District Commissioner is also the head of the authority structure in villages, thus her/his roles combine both traditional and formal processes of dispute resolution. A villager seeking assistance at the District Commissioner's office must have some authority in the form of an introductory/referral letter from the village/group headman and traditional authority. Land disputes and inheritance issues, especially where the deceased died interstate and was employed at the time of death, are the most common cases from the villages that the District Commissioners deal with. People in the study indicated that inheritance issues are taken up with the District Commissioner's office in order to ensure that the property left behind by a deceased person should be disposed of fairly. Interviews with District Commissioners and other stakeholders at the district level confirmed this fact. The role of the District Commissioner in disposing property of the deceased is entrenched in the laws of Malawi. The law that deals with such matters is referred to as the Wills and Inheritance Act. In its present form, the Wills and Inheritance Act does not protect women and has greatly contributed to the problem of property dispossession. Nationally, the Wills and Inheritance Act does not recommend a uniform inheritance system but rather prescribes a sharing system based on the type of marriage. For matrilineal marriages, the Wills and Inheritance Act prescribes that the surviving wife and children should inherit 40% of the property while the rest goes to the deceased's traditional heirs. The proportions are to be stored on a 50:50 basis in patrilineal marriages. In both matrilineal and patrilineal marriages, all household property is supposed to go to the surviving spouse and children such that the proportions are the formula for sharing out non-household property.

While the Wills and Inheritance Act was designed to protect the welfare of women and children by allocating all household property to them, it is in the non-household property where true wealth lies. It is this property that determines the long-term welfare of the wife and children and yet that is where the Wills and Inheritance Act defers to custom on how the property is to be shared. It is clear that this practice arises from the perception that the spousal relationship does not entitle women to much inheritance.

We consider it therefore imperative that this perception must be changed and the law reviewed so as to make the spousal relationship a basis for inheritance (Ngwira, et. al 2002:113). It must be noted that the Wills and Inheritance Act is not gender sensitive in its current form as it assumes only the man as the breadwinner thus simply addresses the issue of inheritance for women while its is silent on men. Granted, it is women who are mostly victims of property dispossession. A national study on *Women's Property and Inheritance Rights in Malawi* has shown that widows are 10 times more likely to experience property dispossession than widowers. When dispossession occurs, women lose 74% of the items of property while men lose 53% of the same (Ngwira, et.al, 2002:112). Since the incidence of will writing is very low in Malawi, we consider it imperative that the Wills and Inheritance Act be strengthened so that a uniform system of inheritance is instituted nationally. In addition, the Wills and Inheritance Act should become gender sensitive and should protect the interests of the surviving spouse (especially women) and children. This is a key element in the effort to combat gender-based violence.

During the study, the research team came across women who had experienced property dispossession as illustrated by these two narratives:

"I found a real man – I mean a real man like the one whose characteristics we have narrated in our discussion. He had three children from his previous marriage. Unfortunately, he got sick, and he decided to give his children from the first marriage their share of his property. We then accumulated some more property together. When he died though, his relatives gave me a tough time. They took from me all his bank account books, including some household items. I did not go to complain to the police because I knew that most of his relatives are better off and that the case would work in their favour. After all, being uneducated, when one goes to complain to the police and other offices, the people in those offices talk in English. You just sit there assuming they are still greeting each other and you are surprised to be told that the case is over without you having been able to follow the proceedings."

"After my husband died in February this year, in March, his relatives came to tell me that the mourning period was over and that I was free to marry someone else if I wanted to. On the day that they told me this, they took everything from the household, including the maize harvest and yet I have four children. I do not get any support from my late husband's family."

Formal Structure

The Police

While the police system represents the formal structure, it intersects with the primary system of justice in some cases, when people in the villages are referred directly to the police by the village head. The following are cases that are taken to the Police: if one is caught stealing for example, in someone's garden, livestock etc.; fighting that results in the drawing of blood; murder; rape; arson; stabbing; keeping a fugitive in one's house; defilement.

The procedure is that the case is first brought to the Chief who then gives the complainant a letter to take to the police for immediate attention and action. During the study, an exception to this practice was found in Mulanje where the process of accessing the police has been politicized. Thus, once the case is brought to the chief, s/he has to inform the party chairman who then writes the referral letter to the Police. These cases are referred to the chairman of the ruling party (UDF) at the village level. This is an illustration of the lack of separation between politics and government. After all, people always hear of the UDF government on the radio, other forms of mass media and through the party's political rallies. People are therefore simply responding to the fact that things will get done if they go through a ruling party structure. However, the system is not the best in a multi-party system where supporters of an opposition party may not get the assistance they need. In one village, the study found that the party chairman actually charges people for services rendered. For example, if it is a case of theft, the chairman demands MK500.00 before he can write the referral letter to the police (MK250.00 each paid for by the complainant and the suspect). It is argued that the chairman should be given the payment for services rendered, in view of the fact that theirs is not a salaried job. This practice acts as an impediment to access to justice for those without money and to supporters of opposition parties.

A female Chief described the cooperation between Chiefs and the local police:

"I had secured the dead body of a woman and held the perpetrator, her husband, in custody. I sent someone to call the police (phone is 3 hours walking distance). They responded that they could not come for lack of transport. The assumed perpetrator escaped – no custody facilities available in village – the dead body had to be buried. The husband/perpetrator is said to still hide in the mountains and is still roaming the area at night eating at his relatives' houses. The chief is still very unhappy that the police neither investigate or try to catch him. The family of the woman are very upset about it all."

The Victim Support Unit

Since 1994 the Malawi Police has embarked on a police reform program that has been mostly supported with funding from the United Kingdom. Part of the reform activities has been the establishment of community policing through which communities participate in the maintenance of law and order in their areas. Victim Support Units fall under the general umbrella of the Community Policing Programme and have received substantial financial support from GTZ. They function as units that provide: counselling, first aid, private interviews and referrals in cases of gender-based violence.

The study focused on the Police Victim Support Unit as a case study of the extent to which people access and utilize formal structures of justice. Officers working in the Victim Support Units were interviewed. In addition, observations were conducted in each of the Victim Support Units in the three districts where the study was conducted. Furthermore, secondary data recorded cases, that the Victim Support Unit handles, were analyzed. Records analyzed for Rumphi covered the period May 2001 to May 2003; the period for Dedza was June 2001 to May 2003, while for Mulanje the data analyzed was from July 2000 to May 2003. The records were often incomplete with data in some columns not having been filled out. The officers explained that recording of the data is often incomplete because they are not always informed of the process and outcome of a case. There is need to develop a systematic way of recording data in all Victim Support Units and to sensitize all Police officers to the importance of the Victim Support Unit. All the same, the present data provides us with important indicators to better direct efforts of the project to eradicate gender-based violence.

The Victim Support Unit handles mostly gender-based violence cases: rape, defilement, divorce, wife battery, property grabbing, general domestic disputes and minor conflicts that may not need the attention of the courts. When a victim gets to the main police counter, they narrate their case and the officers at the counter determine if the case should be referred to the Victim Support Unit. Rape cases are first referred to the Criminal Investigation Department and later to the Victim Support Unit for an interview and counselling. Unless officers at the counter are aware of the role of the Victim Support Unit and have been sensitized in gender issues, it is likely that many cases needing the attention of the Victim Support Unit will slip through the system. There is a need to have a Victim Support Unit screening officer right at the main counter where cases are first presented to the Police.

Victim Support Unit Rumphi Town. Interview with Barbara Mhango from Rumphi
Magistrate's Court by Linda Semu and Stella Ndau. Photo: Maria Saur

The Victim Support Units are located away from the main Police unit in
order to give victims privacy and assurance. Currently, they are limited by
inadequate space, staffing and resources. However, most of the staff working
in the Victim Support Units are committed to their job and have grasped the
idea behind the setting up of the units. Some of them have had on the job
training and exposure to gender issues and counselling. During observations
in one particular Victim Support Unit, the research team noted that people
who came to the Victim Support Unit were told, *"You are welcome"* instead
of the usual *"What can I do for you?"* This is very critical in putting victims
at ease and complainants, especially for rural residents that tend to be
intimidated by the formality and alien nature of the processes of the formal
system of justice.

Due to the broad nature of cases that the Victim Support Unit handles it
also acts as a referral Centre where cases are referred to appropriate departments (government and NGOs) at the district level. Coordination among the
various departments dealing with related issues exists. In all three districts,
there is the district executive committee, a coordinating body of all government and non-governmental organizations operating there. In addition, Victim
Support Unit and the Police in general deal directly with the hospital through

cross-referrals. The main action taken by the Victim Support Unit in the cases that were recorded is referral to the hospital (table 8). In Rumphi, the Victim Support Unit is part of the committee on Victim Support Services that comprises: Police, Hospital, District Commissioner, Social Welfare, the Department of Youth, the Magistrate Court and NGOs. In Dedza, a gender network exists to which the Victim Support Unit officers belong. Even though the Victim Support Unit was established in 2000, it hasn't been very active in Mulanje until recently. In May 2003 the unit was allocated its own space and is currently located in a former veterinary holding cell for dogs. Space is limited and there is need to refurbish the office. That notwithstanding, the officers show a lot of enthusiasm for their work and liaise with other related departments at the district level.

Police Action	Rumphi	Dedza	Mulanje
Referred to hospital	115	-	7
Referred to hospital and suspect cautioned	3	-	-
Case-file opened	2	55	-
Case-file opened, victim referred to hospital	58	41	-
Suspect arrested & victim sent to hospital	3	-	18
Victim sent to hospital, file closed	-	-	11
Case file opened and referred to Magistrate/court	1	11	-
Case-file opened, victim referred to hospital, pending court	-	14	-
Suspect Arrested	-	6	9
Counselling	2	11	7
Investigation to start / on-going	1	-	3
Accused arrested but out on bail	1	-	-
Case withdrawn	-	7	6
File closed	-	2	-

Table 8: Action taken by Police on cases reported at Victim Support Unit by district, July 2000 - June 2003, Source: Victim Support Unit Records

Information obtained from interviews and records shows that the main strategy adopted by the Victim Support Unit in handling cases is that of counselling and giving advice. This is in response to the need by victims to have their abusive partners simply cautioned rather than put in custody. Officers indicated that in most wife battery cases, the women withdraw cases due to pressure from friends and family(ies) as well as due the fact that their intention of bringing up the case is to show the man that they are fed up with his abusive behaviour but not necessarily to have him jailed. This highlights the need to synchronize approaches to dispute resolution as represented by the primary system and the formal justice system. The main aim of the primary system of justice is to restore harmony rather than the attribution of blame which is the basis of the formal system.

Data from the villages shows that there are a lot of gender-based violence cases that occur in the villages. However, due to the existing procedure for dispute resolution that exists in the villages, most of the cases do not reach the Victim Support Unit thus pointing to the need to strengthen the structures at the primary level. In addition, the Victim Support Units are located in towns which are inaccessible to most villagers. As indicated in table 8, it takes on average, three hours for villagers to walk to the district police station in Mung'anya and Nyamaduna in Rumphi; and Kukada and Sambatiyao in Mulanje respectively. It takes on average one hour for Kuluya residents and half an hour for Kapesi residents in Dedza to walk to the Police station. The Victim Support Unit is a good idea but its impact is limited to a specific catchment area in town. For those that are able to access the service, the Victim Support Unit can act as one of the key strategies in combating gender-based violence. The Victim Support Unit can also be used as a means of sensitizing communities on gender-based violence through the sensitization campaigns that it conducts in liaison with the Community Policing Program and some NGOs. For those that are able to access the Victim Support Unit, the majority of the clients are females. As is indicated in table nine and ten, age and gender are important variables in the profile of the victim and suspects of gender-based violence. Thus, most victims tend to be females while the majority of the suspects are male. In both cases, the victims and suspects tend to be younger, pointing to the need to target specific age groups in the program. Thus, most of the female victims under the age of thirteen are victims of defilement, pointing to the need for special measures to protect the girl child within the broad program of eradicating gender-based violence.

Age Range	Rumphi				Dedza				Mulanje			
	Suspects		Victims		Suspects		Victims		Suspects		Victims	
	M	F	M	F	M	F	M	F	M	F	M	F
< 13	3	-	1	8	-	-	-	14	1	-	-	21
14-19	12	1	12	12	9	2	-	29	5	1	-	10
20-25	26	2	25	22	23	3	1	44	9	-	-	14
26-30	27	-	17	15	10	2	-	24	13	-	-	3
31-35	13	3	18	6	6	1	3	21	8	-	2	3
36-40	5	1	9	3	4	-	-	9	5	-	-	-
41-45	3	-	6	3	2	2	-	4	2	-	-	2
46-50	3	1	5	1	2	-	-	3	-	1	-	-
51+	6	-	8	5	3	1	-	13	3	-	2	-
Age not recorded	64	3	5	5	81	4	-	28	3	-	-	5
Groups/ Gangs	-	-	-	-	4	-	-	-	-	-	-	-
TOTAL	204	11	116	80	144	15	4	189	49	2	4	58

Table 9: Characteristics of suspects and victims by age, gender and district, July 2000-June 2003. Discrepancy between number of suspects and victims due to recording errors

Source: Victim Support Unit Records.

Type of Offence	Rumphi		Dedza		Mulanje	
	Male on Female	Male on Male	Male on Female	Male on Male	Male on Female	Male on Male
Indecent Assault	8	1	9	-		-
Assault	51	73	69	1	9	-
Breach of Peace	1	-	2	-	3	1
Theft	2	-	6	-	-	-
Defilement	6	-	10	-	21	-
Rape & Attempted Rape	4	-	17	-	17	-
Incest by Males	1	-	-	-	-	-
Property Grabbing	3	-	1	-	1	-
Unlawful Wounding	4	42	61	1	3	-
Failure to Support Wife	1	-	-	-	-	-
Abduction	-	1		-	1	-

Accidental Shooting	-	-	1	-	-	-
Domestic Violence	-	-	7	-	1	-
Procuring Abortion	-	-	1	-	-	-
Murder	-	-	1	-	2	2
Intimidation	-	-	4	-	1	-
Complaint against Police	-	-	2	2	-	-
Official Corruption	-	-	1	-	-	-
Use of Insulting Language	-	-	1	-	-	-
Armed robbery	-	-	-	-	1	-
Offence not stated	-	-	2	-	-	-

Table 10: Type and number of offences perpetrated by males on females and males on fellow males, by district, July 2000-June 2003. **Source:** Victim Support Unit Records.

People's assessment of the structures of justice

In all the villages where data was collected, people expressed satisfaction with the immediate rather than the more distant systems of justice. This view was also corroborated by various stakeholders that were interviewed at the district administration headquarters, the Boma, in each of the three districts (see appendix 1 as a list of individuals interviewed at the Boma). They were all of the view that a project to combat gender-based violence will have to be based at the village level with chiefs, ankhoswe and various pace setters as strategic partners. Generally, they expressed concern over deteriorating social and economic conditions generally and in particular, the increasing incidence and depth of poverty. Villagers associated the breakdown in social conditions with the adoption of "democracy" that has incorrectly been taken to mean the "right to do what one wants". The villagers also blamed the government for adopting policies such as the removal of fertilizer subsidies and reducing access to loans and fertilizer that have resulted in increasing poverty in rural areas. Most complaints against the police involved corruption, the granting of bail and the 48-hours rule, prompting one participant to ask: *"Where does the money posted for bail go? Who gets that money?"* The villagers' panoramic assessment of the various institutions is presented here:

Chiefs and Ankhoswe

"We find the chiefs and the ankhoswe as the most reliable institutions here in the villages."

"Here in the villages, the chiefs are the most reliable because they are right there and they see and quickly respond to issues as they arise"

"We quickly rush to the chief whenever a problem arises because s/he is like our eyes: responding to any problem that crops up."

The Police

"The police are helpful but they are very corrupt."

"Before a case is heard, you see the suspect being released from Police custody"

"The police does not follow up and conclude cases: For example, my former husband stabbed me on the neck, in the ribs and on the butt. I lost a lot of blood and I had to get a transfusion at the hospital. My ex was only in Police custody for three days after which he was released and there has never been any follow up since then."

"How can case files go missing at the police station without proper follow up and disciplining the responsible officers? All this has to do with some officers being corrupt."

"Some of the police officers are the ones that connive with thieves, armed robbers and drug peddlers."

"The police have now abrogated on their responsibilities since they are just relying on the Community Police yet the latter are not trained police officers and lack the appropriate equipment."

The Government/Boma

"Tends to favour the rich and urban elite."

"All development initiatives are initially introduced in towns before they are taken to the people in the villages."

"We the villagers are not able to organize ourselves. We do not have the language to articulate our interests."

"For one to get a job, you have to be related to, or know a politician."

"Leadership positions are reserved for the better off even though they do not assist us in our needs. For example, in our area, a candidate for the position of Member of Parliament was brought in from Britain instead of choosing a local person."

"If there is a case to answer, it always works out in favour of the rich even if they are in the wrong."

"The government does not deliver on its promises."

"It promises to assist orphans. List of names of eligible children have been drawn up and presented to the DC and yet nothing has happened."

"The whole process of development work and aid for the needy has been politicized."

"For example, it is only members of the UDF party who get food hand-outs. When a rice donation was brought to the village, it was only the UDF supporters who got some rations."

"The introduction surtax, high fertilizer prices, the general increase in the prices of basic commodities and the closure of some companies such as ADMARC and Malawi Railways have resulted in the loss of jobs and the associated increase in poverty."

"Most government officials are corrupt."

"For example, we have to pay MK7.00 in order to collect firewood in the government forest. However, some guards issue fake receipts while others have sex with those women who are not able to pay for the permit."

Hospitals

"Some people cannot afford the MK15.00 health card and even though it is supposed to be optional, some health personnel refuse to attend to those that do not have it."

"There are no drugs and health personnel at the government hospitals: the other day I took a child there but I didn't get any medication. I ended up having to buy the drugs."

"Women who go to deliver at government hospitals are treated badly. Just this year, three women from this village were on separate occasions beaten up by a nurse when they went to the hospital for delivery. And that lady over there had her daughter deliver on her own because the nurse refused to attend to her during labour."

The Education Sector

"Teachers should stop impregnating our daughters."

"Even though there is free primary education, there are other costs that make it expensive. In addition, most parents cannot afford to pay the fees for secondary schooling."

"Teachers are not paid on time as a result they are not committed in their job."

Members of Parliament

"They only come to the villages when they are campaigning and trying to get our votes but once they are elected as Members of Parliament they stop coming to the villages."

Analysis of Findings and Recommendations

Nkhanza or Gender-Based Violence?

The study has shown that the English notion of violence does not correspond with the concept of Nkhanza in Chichewa. Violence has to be translated as Nkhanza. Yet the word Nkhanza in itself has a far broader meaning. Nkhanza does not clearly distinguish between physical and psychological cruelty and abuse, both are called Nkhanza. This has broad implications. People perceive psychological cruelty, structural violence and various other forms of abuse as seriously as physical harm.

This brings us to the first cultural misunderstanding: The western/ northern approach – perpetuated by the donor community – distinguishes clearly between violence as physical harm inflicted on a person and other forms of cruelty and abuse. The western/northern approach to combat gender-based violence seems to give physical violence more emphasis, thus programs with the emphasis on physical harm are induced and funded.

The various ethnic groups/peoples/tribes in Malawi are all approaching this topic in their own cultural context. What they have in common, though, is that physical harm and other forms of cruelty and abuse cannot clearly be distinguished, certainly not in a hierarchical order as the western approach suggests, considering physical violence the worst.

For these reasons we have decided to use the term *Nkhanza* in the text, to cover the broader concept.

Given this understanding one could conclude that the English title of the CBGV Project (Combating Gender-Based Violence) does not describe nor encompass what Malawians want to be addressed when they are 'combating' Nkhanza.

Nkhanza the norm

The overall picture portrays a country in which physical abuse seems to be as much the norm as non-physical forms of Nkhanza. Physical violence is seen as an almost unavoidable and unquestioned tool for solving conflict in general. We learned in the interviews, that the President of the country, Dr.

Bakili Muluzi, is known to beat up his wife regularly and occasionally vice versa. Does he just represent a normative behaviour or is he a role model or even both?

The fact that corporal punishment in prisons, schools and even hospitals is therefore normal practice reflects that beating is a normative, accepted and condoned way of interaction in Malawi. Thus even if it were wished for – which it is in many cases – there are few cultural patterns available on how physical violence during conflict can be avoided.

Women, men and children have internalized the fact that 'educational beating' is a necessary measure to become a responsible adult, or a wife for that matter. Herein lies the challenge for finding and implementing strategies and tactics to combat Nkhanza in Malawi.

The Impact of Economic Factors

Every person we spoke to was convinced that the direct economic situation causes a lot of Nkhanza, thus it was felt, that an improved economic situation would ease Nkhanza in all its forms on all levels.

The findings confirm this to some extent only. It clearly shows that the difficulties of ensuring a regular food supply in the domestic sphere are an enormous source of tension and therefore most regularly lead to all forms of Nkhanza.

This was unanimously stated by all our 'dialogue-partners' and certainly holds a lot of truth. But it can also be seen that economic empowerment alone is not a guarantee of less Nkhanza. It can even lead to the opposite effect as it was observed in Rumphi, one of the more prosperous regions of Malawi. (The same can be confirmed worldwide in western, northern and eastern countries with better economic situations than Malawi, where domestic violence is still very common).

In Rumphi District we observed how prosperity could even work to the disadvantage of women and empower men to inflict even more Nkhanza on their partners. The male tobacco farmers use their cash income that was generated by selling tobacco and mostly produced jointly with the wife to cheat on their spouse(s) in every sense of the word as men and women alike explained. The deprivation of knowledge and education meant that many women were not able to distinguish between US Dollars and Kwacha on the auction floor certificate – their partners gravely abused this.

But the adverse is also true. Dire poverty, hunger and starvation led to increased Nkhanza in the afflicted villages – probably inevitably so. Since, if a person has to fight for food to survive, the inhibitions that normally prevent abuse of another person falter for the sake of one's own survival and that of one's family. This is, so to speak, 'normal' human behaviour, informed by the wish not to die. We came to understand that in its various ways in the villages affected by severe food shortage and starvation in the year 2002. People saw themselves as forced to steal crops from each other's fields, granaries and houses, harming and killing each other in the process. This hardship led to mass-graves in the villages and to unspeakable traumatization of the surviving adults and children.

We can conclude that economic empowerment is a factor that could help to reduce Nkhanza, but will not do so on its own. Economic empowerment can reduce Nkhanza, only if it goes hand in hand with strategies to establish change of behaviour patterns. This could include education strategies, the provision of information to make women more aware of their legal rights and economic measures such as access to land so that they can provide for themselves.

Economic empowerment – but only if it is done in a gendered way – can be assumed to change the perpetuation of Nkhanza considerably. If women gain more independence, economically they have a better chance to get out of volatile/cruel relationships without fear for their survival. That this holds true can be shown by comparing the Southern districts with the Northern ones. The extent and forms (meaning economic betrayal) of Nkhanza become less, or certainly less extreme and not encompassing the whole life sphere' for women, in the matrilineal and matrilocal villages in the South. As described in our study, the women in matrilocal families are not economically dependant on their Nkhanza inflicting partners. The economic 'hindrances/obstacles' to leave an abusive relationship are much reduced. The women's standard of living might still go down considerably if the husband is 'chased away' (which she has a right to do) but she is not without means to support herself and her children.

Women in patrilineal and patrilocal villages have to take this risk though, to lose "bed, bread and children". They are threatened with losing their children and the means to support them when they consider ending violent relationship. In the South, in the predominantly matrilocal, more economically prosperous areas the women do not have to fear to lose their 'daily bread and bed' so to speak, if she stands up for herself; in that sense she is much more empowered. A clear difference between south and north was found.

Although people in the North are statistically better educated it has no effect on the well being of women, contradicting so the common concept that sheer education will improve women's lives. Our findings clearly show that the women in the best-educated part of Malawi are the worst off; 'trapped slaves' and 'living on panadol' as they described themselves.

Beating – An Accepted Form of Conflict Resolution

Although there are considerable cultural variations, cultural patterns throughout the country allow physical abuse to deal with disagreements, misunderstandings or conflicts. Though the ideal is nonetheless, apart from educational beating, that physical violence and other forms of nkhanza should be avoided.

Yet the acceptance of educational beating between adults indicates that one of them is not seen as an adult with equal rights but rather as a subordinate minor – to be educated and ruled over. If a woman who is supposed to prepare the food for the family has to ask the husband about how much and which food can be used, under the threat of repercussions, she is certainly not considered an equal partner at all.

There seem to be very few 'tools at hand' to deal with conflict in a constructive way, no means to debate controversial issues 'peacefully' – hardly a vision that this could even be possible. This is confirmed by the fact that men consider themselves entitled to beat, even if they are only verbally questioned. On the other hand we learnt in interviews with those involved in counselling – 'the aunties', 'the uncles', the ankhoswe, the chiefs, and church leaders – that tools for non-violent resolutions were not available. People could hardly imagine that such tools and means exist. When asked how they dealt with the Nkhanza cases, the most common answer was: "We tell them to not do it again and to love each other." That this hasn't had any effect or worked can be seen in so far as nkhanza is still around although all authorities have been preaching against it. To deal with conflict in a non-violent way is a not so easy skill to be learnt and acquired; it does not come naturally as can be clearly seen in children but in adults world-wide too. Non-violent conflict resolution is on the agenda but not widely practiced, neither in the political nor in the private sphere. The latter two inform each other, though.

The chief has one additional measure, that of punishment. This does at times have a temporary effect, but is also based on creating fear and humiliation – not a good base for reconciliation.

The ankhoswe are generally expected to encourage endurance – which mostly means women enduring more abuse, since the failure of a marriage is also seen as their failure. After all, beating is seen as 'the oil of a marriage' as a traditional wedding song puts it.

Change is on the way though since Ben Michael, a Malawian composer whom we briefly interviewed, is now singing: 'don't beat her she is so beautiful'. It may be noted that he does not rule out beating as such but just to not harm her beauty!

The Psychological Impact of Nkhanza

In psychological terms one can conclude that all parties have internalized a hierarchical way of interaction. This means, that there are superiors who can impose their wishes and minors/inferiors who have to endure the physical violence and other forms of Nkhanza. That this is indeed internalized and rationalized can be seen by the fact that the abused, mostly women and children, are defending the 'educational beating' showing that they themselves think this is the only way to learn and to be taught. This mechanism is called identification with the aggressor – *"he beats me so I could learn and not do it the next time again ..."* The anger and fury is mostly suppressed to an unconscious level where it is nonetheless active and can lead to psychosomatic illnesses and/or cause auto-destructive behaviour of which we have seen a lot. One example is he case study of Mrs. Phiri, the young woman who's feet had swollen up so she could not walk anymore to school where every day someone was waiting to beat her up. No clear medical reason was found for the swelling of the feet. So, by not being able to walk to school, the beating was avoided but the much cherished education was lost. This – unconscious – conflict resolution has a rather self-destructive element. The beating is avoided but her career is thereby destroyed.

Another example concerns back-pain, which nearly all women complained about, principally the ones from the North, the most powerless in Malawi. While hard work is certainly a factor in this, there is most likely a psychological element too, since it corresponds with the psychosomatic theory, that back pain is often a result of suppressed aggression on the verge of being acted out. The assumption is that one's own pain prevents one from lashing out and therefore 'helps' to conform to cultural patterns i.e. not fighting back or fight at all. So the ability to conform – although one is burning with fury and anger – comes at the price of pain; one pays a self-destructing price to be able to deal with the conflict.

This is to mention only a few of the many possibilities of how repressed anger can or could have manifested itself in the women we interviewed.

The children however, were very clear in their interpretation of things. They strongly felt that if their mothers are beaten by the father she acts it out on the kids and inflicts Nkhanza on them.

This is of course a very common form of dealing with one's powerlessness: if one cannot fight back because the aggressor is, in reality or perception, too powerful, one acts out the tension on a weaker person, in this case the child.

It is sometimes interpreted that men become violent against their wives because they feel powerless in society in general, or some place in their life (H. Moore 1998). With the data collected in this study, we would not support this theory so far.

Recommendations

As shown in this study, to act out one's impulse i.e. hit or abuse when one feels questioned, hurt or challenged, is the norm; it is sanctioned by society.

This form of conflict resolution is accepted, at times promoted (family, school, hospital, prison), with no other means available for dealing with aggressive impulses.

This is confirmed by the fact that a lot of activists against Gender-based violence Nkhanza seem convinced that preaching against it, is all that can be done and needs to be done. It shows that they themselves as members of the Malawi society have no concept, that other forms of behaviour can and must be learnt, trained and practiced, to address stressful aggressive conflict situations.

This vicious circle can only be addressed and tackled by profound awareness raising of human rights, the right to bodily integrity, and by profound empowered strategies on an economic and educational level. Furthermore mechanisms have to be introduced to deal with conflict. In that respect, training measures have to encompass all parties involved. The vision has to be promoted, that less Nkhanza makes life more enjoyable for all. This is a very high goal but a very conducive one.

Therefore, all traditionally legitimized, religious and (non)-governmental people and institutions should be trained to promote the issue in a practical way. The ankhoswe and the churches must at the same time become flexible in regarding divorce as a means of conflict resolution. As one chief wisely remarked - she meanwhile knows who has to be divorced immediately to prevent the worst happening. The new skills to be acquired regarding peaceful conflict resolution should be 'debating skills', skills of interaction in its broadest sense. Furthermore it has to be recognized that newly acquired skills of interaction can often only be applied in a new relationship!

Since it is commonly acknowledged that all change only happens at a rather slow pace – parallel intermediate prevention activities are proposed. Some chiefs and ankhoswe, for example, have a reporting system where perpetuators have to show up on a regular basis. This could be expanded and/or new kind of neutral discreet 'reporting /supervising' committees could be formed to prevent public humiliation which is mostly counterproductive in the long run. 'Public shaming' is at times practiced in the villages, but with little long-term effect as we have learnt.

Legislative level

Parallel to the interventions at village and family level, steps have to be taken on a legislative level. Although physical violence is outlawed on a one to one relationship, corporal punishment in government institutions like schools, hospitals and prisons is common practice thus most prevalent and legal. This has to be addressed otherwise very conflicting messages are being conveyed.

We found that most people hoped, that the new President, who is going to be elected in May 2004, will address this issue.

The women of the North should be eligible to land ownership and hence economic independence. This could perhaps be addressed in relation to the issue of *lobola* payment.

Structural violence

In the eyes of all our dialogue partners and interviewees, the inaccessibility to law, information and knowledge in general, formed the base of structural violence. All persons talked with on the village level had regrets about their not being able to finish their education due to lack of funds. All wanted to study and learn more in the hope to improve their personal and economic situation. Yet in all cases there were no means to pursue this.

Generally, we found that there was a lack of knowledge about what kind of help is provided from the government level. Many people for example were not aware of the existence of a 'Community Welfare Officer' at Boma level, let alone that they could turn to her/him when support was needed. The same applies to other governmental extension workers, their mere existence was often not known. Yet again men were better informed than women.

Human rights

In some villages, mostly in the South again, human rights were already on the agenda. Nkhanza was regarded as conflicting with human rights but in general there was no awareness of it. Awareness raising in that respect was seen by many a chief as an absolute necessity – to approach the field of gender-based Nkhanza.

The fact that Malawi has signed the Peking Protocol and various other international agreements is hardly known, let alone the implications it has for the rights of every Malawian citizen.

Networking

As worldwide studies about violence against women have shown, the indicator that mattered most in terms of moving from a violence inflicted life to a non-violent one, was the existence of networks. (Purna Sen, London 2003)

Networks that affected people can turn to; networks that provide 'social control' i.e. outlaw at least physical violence in the village and interfere if necessary; networks where women and men can learn how to interact differently and practice with the help of peer-group supporters.

Conclusion

The study has found that people's definition of *"nkhanza"* is broader than the western concept of violence and is based on inter-personal relationships. As a broad concept that covers all forms of abuse, the people's understanding of *"nkhanza"* implies the inseparability of rights. Any form of abuse is therefore a violation of rights. Most importantly, the study has found that the dispute resolution mechanism that is readily accessible and most reliable for most rural people is at the village level. The traditional systems are proximate, flexible and faster in responding to problems as they arise. On the other hand, the formal system is viewed as being alien, unreliable and inaccessible.

The study recognizes that many attempts are being made and have been made in the past to eradicate nkhanza/gender-based violence. However, most of the interventions have had little impact, probably due to problems in targeting. In view of experiences from other projects and the knowledge acquired in this study, the project to eradicate nkhanza/gender-based violence will have to adopt a multi faceted approach with special effort and emphasis placed at the village level in rural areas where the majority of Malawians live.

Interviewees at Boma Level

RUMPHI

May 21st, 2003	R.E. Phiri – Community Development Officer D. H. Sikwese – Assistant Social Welfare Officer
May 22nd, 2003	Mrs. Ngosi – Inspector Victim Support Unit
May 23rd, 2003	M. Mulenga – Community Development Assistant for Bale – Nyamaduna Area. H. Simwaka – Social Welfare Assistant
May 29th, 2003	M.K.D. Chilinda – Labour Officer S.F. Kondowe – Clerical Officer C.R. Mwalwanda – Orthopaedic Clinical Officer

DEDZA

June 5th, 2003	Mrs. Howahowa – Sub-Inspector, Victim Support Unit S.M.G. Chimaliro – First Grade Magistrate
June 6th, 2003	B. Maenje – Labour Assistant
June 10th, 2003	A. Mtengula – District Commissioner
June 11th, 2003	S.A.N. Masoo – Community Development Officer B. M Kapuchi – Social Welfare Assistant A.G. Chimbali – Social Welfare Assistant P.B. Mengezi – Community Development Assistant F. Phiri – Community Development Assistant. B. Chibambo – Project Manager Concern Universal.
June 12th, 2003	J. Chidothi – Project Coordinator – CCJP District Health Officer

MULANJE

June 20th, 2003   *   H. Twabi – District Commissioner

June 23rd, 2003   *Mrs. M. Malemia – Sub-Inspector, Victim Support Unit
*Mrs. Nyirenda – Sergeant, Victim Support Unit
*C.Jonazi Nguleti – Senior Community Development Assistant

June 25th, 2003   *Mr. Phiri – Senior Clerical Officer
*Mr. Thumba – Clerical Officers, Magistrates' Office
*Chikakuda – Clerical Officers, Magistrates' Office.
*G. Mothisa – District Assistant Labour Officer
*Fweta – Labour Assistant
*M.T. Duwe – Labour Assistant

References

Chirwa, W. et. al, 1999. Violence and Social Injustice Against Women in the Workplace. Vol 1: Main Report, Study Findings and Recommendations.

Chirwa, W. & R. Poeschke, 1998. *The Challenge of Democracy in Malawi: Socio-Anthropological Conditions. Study Report and Recommendations.* Lilongwe: Malawi-German Program for Democracy and Decentralization (GTZ).

International Organization for Development, 1999: Primary Safety, Security and Access to Justice Systems in Rural Malawi. Final report of research Findings and Responses form Stakeholder Workshop. Lilongwe: DFID/MASSAJ Program.

Kakhongwe, P. & E. Mkandawire, 1999: *Malawi Rape and Defilement Study.* Zomba, University of Malawi- Center for Social Research.

Malawi Government, 2002: Malawi Poverty Reduction Strategy Paper- Main Report & Annexes. Lilongwe.

Malawi Government, 2002. *National Strategy to Combat Gender-Based Violence 2002-2006.* Lilongwe: Ministry of Gender and Community Services.

Malawi Government, 2000: *National Gender Policy 2000-2005.* Lilongwe, Ministry of Gender and Community Services.

Malawi Government, 2000: *The Constitution of the Republic of Malawi.* Lilongwe, Design Printers.

Mastwijk, Sabine, 1999: Violence against Women: Findings and Conclusions of a Study conducted under CSC- MUCIP in Mzuzu, Malawi. Lilongwe, CSC and GTZ.

Moore, Henrietta, 1998: *A Passion for Difference.* London.

National Economic Council, 2002: Qualitative Impact Monitoring of the Poverty Alleviation Policies and Programs in Malawi. Vol 1: Survey Findings. Lilongwe,

National Economic Council, 2000: Profile of Poverty in Malawi, 1998: Poverty Analysis of the Malawi Integrated Household Survey, 1997-98. Lilongwe, National Economic Council – Poverty Monitoring.

National Statistical Office & ORC Macro, 2001: *Malawi Demographic and Health Survey 2000.* Zomba, Malawi & Calverton, Maryland, U.S.A.

Phiri, I.; L. Semu, F. Nankhuni & N. Madise, 1995. Violence against Women in Educational Institutions: The Case of Sexual Harassment and Rape at Chancellor College Campus. Zomba, Chancellor College.

United Nations System in Malawi, 2001: *Common Country Assessment of Malawi, 2001 Report.* Lilongwe, The Development Center.

SADC Heads of State or Government, 1997: *SADC Declaration on Gender and Development*, Blantyre.

Saur, M, 1991: Chewa- und Ngoni Aspekte von Frauenleben in Malawi, Frankfurt/M., Germany, unpublished thesis.

Sen, P. 2003: Public Lecture at London School of Economics and Political Science, Developing Studies Institute, England

Contact Addresses

Maria Saur, Social Anthropologist/Consultant, London, England

e-mail:mmsaur@yahoo.co.uk

Linda Semu, Sociologist/Consultant Zomba, Malaŵi/Indiana, USA

e-mail: lsemu@indiana.edu.

Stella Hauya Ndau, Linguist/Consultant Zomba, Malawi

e-mail: shauya@chanco.unima.mw

www.ingramcontent.com/pod-product-compliance
Lightning Source LLC
Chambersburg PA
CBHW021838020426
42334CB00014B/679